**ACTON CENTRAL STATION
BOOK SWAP**
Please take this book placed
here by your
local community association
www.churchfield.org

Do please put this book back on
the shelf after you have read it,
for other travelers to enjoy.

THE QUILT ROOM

THE QUILT ROOM

PATCHWORK AND QUILTING WORKSHOPS

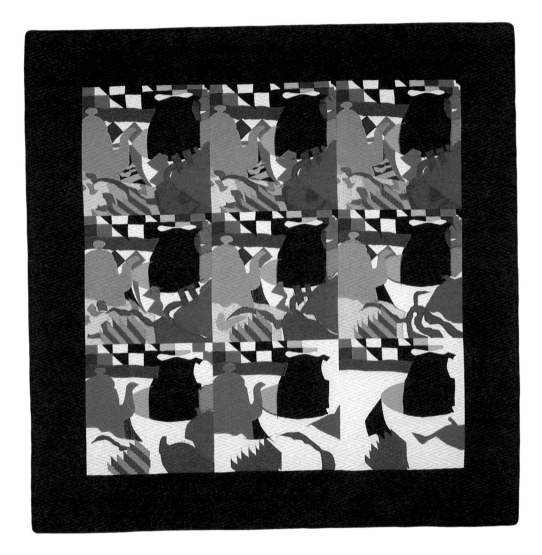

compiled by

Pam Lintott and Rosemary Miller

Note: Accurate conversions from imperial to metric measurements have been given wherever possible but quilters should follow one set of measurements throughout a project.

First published in 1992
by Charles Letts & Co Ltd
Letts of London House
Parkgate Road
London SW11 4NQ

Reprinted 1992

Designed and produced by Rosemary Wilkinson
4 Lonsdale Square, London N1 1EN

Art editor: Frances de Rees
Illustrators: Richard Hawke; Mary Tomlin
Editor: Eleanor van Zandt

© Charles Letts & Co Ltd 1992

All our rights reserved. No part of this publication may be reproduced, stored in a retrieval system, or transmitted, in any form or by any means, electronic, mechanical, photocopying, recording or otherwise, without the prior permission in writing of the publishers.

A CIP catalogue record for this book is available from the British Library

'Letts' is a registered trademark of Charles Letts & Co Limited

ISBN 1 85238 164 7

Typeset by Fakenham Photosetting Ltd, Fakenham, Norfolk

Printed in Great Britain by Butler & Tanner Ltd, Frome and London

Cover photograph: "Snakeskin" by Rita Humphry
Photograph page 1: "Jubilee Terrace" by Dorothy Stapleton
Title page photograph: "Pink Teapot" by Pauline Burbidge
Photograph page 6: "Milky Way" by Pam Lintott & Rosemary Miller

Contents

Introduction

The Quilt Room, our shop in the heart of southern England, celebrated its 10th anniversary in September 1991. It has grown steadily in popularity, so that two years ago we moved to larger premises. Now we have the shop downstairs and a studio above where two or three workshops on patchwork and quilting are held every week during the winter. We persuade tutors to come from far and wide and we never cease to be amazed at their knowledge, skill and enthusiasm. Places at the workshops are in great demand and there is always a waiting list. And so the idea of the book was born.

Here is a selection of those workshops each written by the tutor concerned. The workshops are part inspiration, part practical instruction. The first workshop covers the basics of patchwork, quilting and appliqué; each of the others explores a special technique with an accompanying project or series of projects. Stunning photographs of the tutors' own quilts accompany their descriptions of the way they work and the step-by-step explanations of the projects are all illustrated with clear and plentiful diagrams.

We hope you enjoy looking at and working from the book as much as we have enjoyed having the tutors at *The Quilt Room.*

Pam Lintott
Rosemary Miller

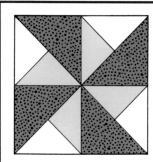

Double Pinwheel

Southern Belle

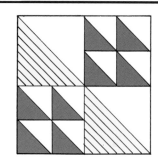

Flock

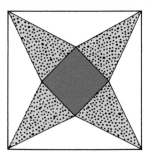

World Without End

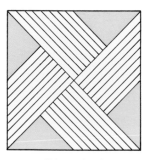

Waterwheel

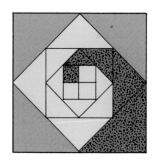

Dutchman's Puzzle

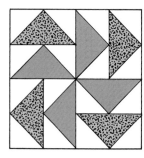

Indiana Puzzle

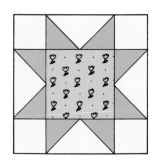

Evening Star

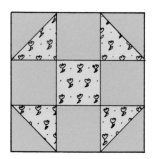

Shoo-Fly

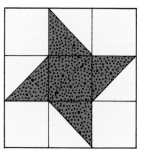

Friendship Star

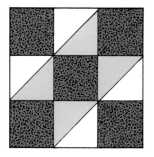

Contrary Wife

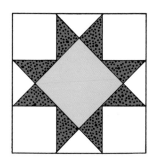

Variable Star

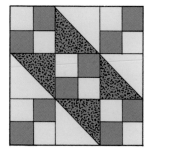

Jacob's Ladder

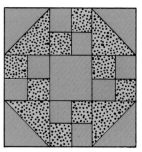

Prairie Queen

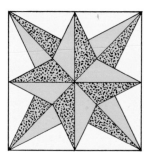

St Louis

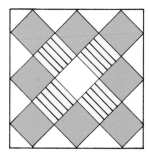

Courthouse Square

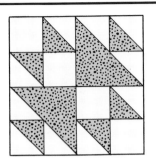

Double X

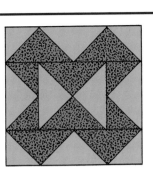

Double Z

Bouquet

Mosaic

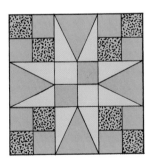

54–40 *or* Fight

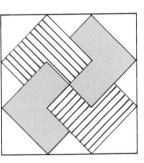

Card Trick

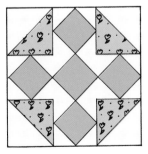

Sawtooth Patch

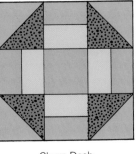

Churn Dash

Basic Techniques

Sharon Chambers

Born in the United States, in Dallas, Sharon Chambers now lives in England, where she teaches patchwork and quilting not only at The Quilt Room but also at her local Adult Education Institute. She attributes her love of sewing to the encouragement of her mother and grandmother – both accomplished needleworkers – and her special interest in making pieced animal quilts to her twenty-five year career as a biological illustrator (for the Smithsonian and the British Museum). Her latest venture is a company producing commercial patchwork patterns.

Starting Off

All you really need to begin quilting are a selection of fabrics, a simple sewing kit, some basic items for drafting and making templates – and enthusiasm. Creating something with your own hands that is both useful and beautiful brings a wonderful feeling of satisfaction that is too good to miss! Relax and put aside any doubts. The sooner you start, the sooner you will feel the warmth of your lovely quilt.

Drawing and Sewing Materials

Needles
Sharps for sewing the patches together and betweens for quilting; choose packs of assorted sizes until you determine your favourite.

Pins
The glass-headed kind are easier to find when dropped.

Thimble
Choose a size that fits comfortably on the middle finger of your dominant hand; many people also wear one on the other hand when quilting, in order to protect the working finger underneath.

Scissors
One pair exclusively for fabric and another for paper.

Rotary Cutter, Cutting Mat and Grid Ruler
The rotary cutter can be used to cut out virtually all patches with straight sides and can cut through multiple layers of fabric. It makes the job of cutting patches quicker and more accurate. It must be used in conjunction with a "self-healing" cutting mat, and a heavy gauge, gridded, plastic ruler, available from the same supplier as the cutter.

Thread
Good-quality cotton or cotton-wrapped polyester sewing thread for hand-stitched patchwork and appliqué; cotton sewing thread for machine stitched patchwork; 100 per cent cotton or cotton-covered polyester quilting thread for hand quilting; 100 per cent cotton quilting thread for machine quilting.

Fabric Markers
2H or H lead pencils for light-coloured fabrics; yellow or white pencils for dark fabrics; a silver pencil will show up on either. Always test markers on each fabric to make sure that they can be removed.

Pencil Sharpener
Only sharply-pointed pencils make accurate lines.

Grid Papers
Graph and isometric papers save time when drafting templates and working out block designs.

Tracing, Cartridge and Coloured Papers
These papers are often recommended in the following workshops for the design stages of quilt planning.

Tape Measure, Ruler, Set Square with 45° angles, Compass, Protractor
For general measuring of templates and fabrics.

Masking Tape
Choose a low-tack variety, especially if it is to be used on fabric, as suggested in the quilting details below.

Clear Template Plastic or Stiff Cardboard and Glue Stick
Plastic templates last indefinitely, but those made from cardboard will need to be replaced once the corners become worn.

Sandpaper
A small piece of very fine sandpaper can be glued to the back of a template to prevent it from slipping out of position while the fabric is being marked.

Quilting Hoop
This helps to keep the quilting sandwich under an even tension while you are hand stitching.

Flannel Board, Cork or Polystyrene Board
Drape a piece of flannelette or felt material over a large pinboard (or any rigid board) and hang this on the wall. Use it for planning the placement of patches in a quilt. Fabric patches will stick to it without pins. A cork or polystyrene-tiled board serves the same purpose, though patches will need to be anchored to it with a pin.

Fabrics
Specific fabrics are discussed in the individual workshops. In general, however, choose 100 per cent cotton dressweight fabrics in light, medium and dark values. Choose any colour or colours that you like, but aim for a variety of patterns, such as large random designs, small all-over florals and geometric prints. Plain fabrics also offer a resting place for the eye among many patterns. Judge your choices from a few paces back before making a final decision, but don't agonize over matching colours *exactly*; variety spices things up and adds richness, whether it be in colour tones or patterns. As a general guideline, I would suggest that you choose a minimum of three fabrics for a patchwork, but six or more can easily be accommodated, especially on a sampler quilt.

Preparation

Prewash all fabrics separately, especially dark or bright colours. Use cool to tepid water and soap flakes or other non-biological detergent without phosphates or bleaching agents. Rinse thoroughly. Some people prefer to work with new, unwashed fabric; if that is your preference, do test each one for colourfastness at least. Test as above, but use only a small square, cut from each fabric. If one fabric continues to run, replace it. Press your fabrics before they are completely dry.

Wadding

I recommend a 2-ounce polyester for a first quilt. This is roughly equivalent to the low-loft batting available in the United States. American quilters also have a choice of thinner, more solid battings, such as needle-punched polyester and bonded cotton batting (which contains 20 per cent polyester) for flatter textures, as well as slightly thicker polyester batting, designated by such terms as "high loft" and "extra loft". In Britain, polyester wadding comes in several thicknesses, up to 6-ounce (suitable only for tied quilts). Pure cotton wadding is also available (note that this should be heavily quilted, every 1½ to 2 in/4 to 5 cm to keep it from bunching up when washed).

Making Templates for Patchwork

Patchwork blocks come in hundreds of patterns, and virtually any size. I start people off on Four-Patch and Nine-Patch designs, both of which will fit easily into a 12 in/30 cm block. These designs are so-called because they are based on a square divided into either four (see top 12 designs, pages 8–9) or nine equal squares (see bottom 12 designs, pages 8–9).

Drafting a block to size is very easy. Let us use the "Shoo-Fly" pattern (see page 8) as an example. For all markings, make sure the pencil is sharp and is held tight against the ruler at an angle of roughly 45° to the paper or fabric (see diagram 1). It causes less distortion if you look directly down on the line as you draw. Being as accurate as possible at each step of the way helps your quilt to piece together smoothly. On graph paper, draw

1

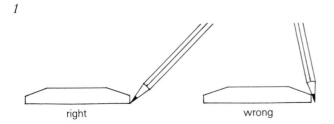

right   wrong

a 12 in/30 cm square, marking the 4 in/10 cm and 8 in/20 cm points on all sides (see diagram 2a). Connect these points horizontally and vertically, dividing the block into nine equal squares (diagram 2b). Next divide the corner squares diagonally as shown in diagram 2c.

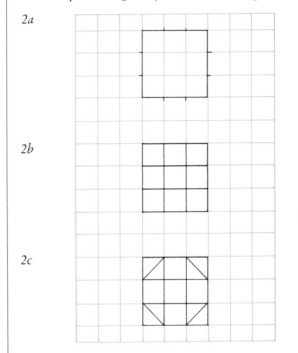

2a

2b

2c

Make one template for each different-sized shape in any block. In the case of "Shoo-Fly", this means making one square and one triangle. If you are using template plastic, lay it rough side down over the drawing and secure with masking tape. Trace both shapes carefully, using a pencil or OHP (overhead projector) pen and ruler, and cut out just inside the marked lines for greater accuracy. If you are using cardboard for your templates, cut out both shapes from the graph paper leaving a margin all around. Glue these to a piece of cardboard, then cut out accurately as above.

Mark each template with the name of the block, its finished size and an identifying letter. Do this on the right side of the template, so that you have an instant check on which way up it should be. This is particularly necessary with asymmetrical shapes. It is also extremely useful to mark each patch with an arrow to show the direction of the fabric grain line (see diagram 3).

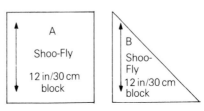

A
Shoo-Fly
12 in/30 cm block

B
Shoo-Fly
12 in/30 cm block

Keep all the templates for a particular block together in an envelope or plastic pocket, labelled with name and size plus a drawing of the block with each patch lettered. For some blocks you may have to cut a number of patches one way and others with the template turned over. Patches that require this treatment are usually marked with the letter "r" after the identifying letter (diagram 4).

4

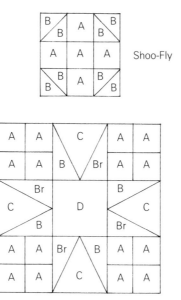

Shoo-Fly

54–40 *or* Fight

Making Templates for Appliqué

Draw the whole block or design actual size on plain paper. Go over it with a black felt-tip pen. Label the different shapes, then, using either tracing paper or clear template plastic, make a copy of each of the separate shapes. Where one shape disappears underneath another, allow extra for the overlap (see diagram 5). Be sure to

5

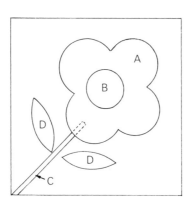

label all templates for identification and keep them together as described above. The direction of the grain line is much more flexible in a patch for appliqué, since you are frequently using curved shapes and it is often more important to use a particular area of pattern on the fabric, than to match the grain.

Planning a Design

The individual workshops which follow give details on planning particular designs and there are hints on fabric choice above. Once you have chosen a particular block for your patchwork, there is still a variety of ways in which the blocks can be arranged to produce a finished quilt. The blocks can be joined edge to edge (see diagram 6a) or with alternate unpieced blocks. This latter method is useful for making a large quilt, as there will be fewer patchwork blocks to piece together, but since the plain blocks need a reasonable amount of quilting to look their best, it is probably no great saving of time. You can also put narrow strips, called "sashing", between blocks and rows (diagram 6b). This separates and frames the different patterns effectively. Alternatively the block can be turned on point (diagram 6c) and all of the above variations tried out.

A cork or flannel-covered board (see page 10) hung on the wall can be of great help in the planning stages. Use it to view fabric choices for the different shapes in a block. You can then stand back from them and see them in different lights.

6a

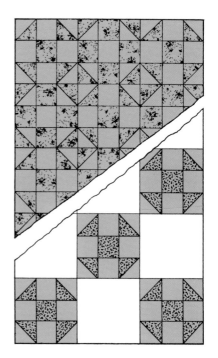

6b

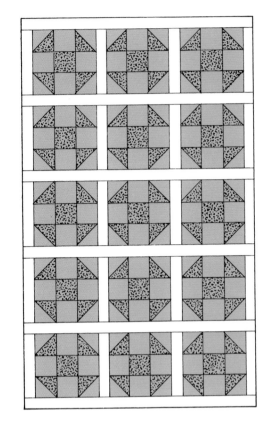

6c

English and American Methods

There are two alternative ways of stitching the patches together. In the English method, a separate paper template without the seam allowance is used for each patch. The seam allowance is folded over to the reverse of the template and basted in place. The patches are then placed right sides together and stitched with a fine oversewing. In the American method, one template which includes the seam allowance is used to mark the fabric and the patches are cut out with seam allowances. The patches are then placed right sides together and stitched by hand or machine. These two methods are explained in detail in "Three-Dimensional Patchwork" on page 101. The details for marking, cutting and piecing patches below are applicable to either method.

Marking and Cutting Fabric for Patchwork

Lay the pressed fabric out flat, wrong side up. Place the template face down on the fabric, lining up the arrow on the template with the grain, wherever possible. You should avoid placing bias edges along the outside of blocks, as it causes them to stretch and distort. If you are using a patterned fabric in such a way that it makes an outer bias edge unavoidable, handle it with care and use stay stitching (a line of stitches just outside the sewing line) to stabilize it. Do not include a selvedge, either in a patch or its seam allowance.

Use a hard lead pencil (see page 10) and draw round the template carefully as described under making the template above. Take particular care at points and corners. If the template slips out of position while you are marking the fabric, try glueing small pieces of fine sandpaper to the wrong side. For the most economical use of fabric, cut the patches close together (see diagram 7). This works well with plain fabric, but you may prefer to select particular areas of pattern on a print fabric and this will govern where you position the template.

7

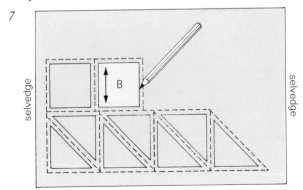

Marking and Cutting Fabric for Appliqué

Lay the pressed fabric right side up. Templates do not include any allowance for the fabric which will be turned under. Place the template on the fabric right side up and mark round it with an appropriate pencil (see page 10). This line represents the fold line. When cutting, allow an extra ³⁄₁₆ in/5 mm all around for turning under. When applying the patches to the background fabric this excess material is folded under so that the pencilled line is just out of sight. However, any area of a patch that will be underneath another in the final design does not need to be turned under.

An alternative method for cutting appliqué patches is to cut a paper template for each patch. Place this on the fabric and cut round it, leaving the turn-under allowance as before. The fabric is then folded over the paper template and basted to it. The paper is removed after the patch has been applied (see below).

Piecing Patchwork

Before beginning to stitch your block, lay out all the patches in their positions within the block. As a general rule, the smallest patches are sewn together first (see diagram 8a); these units are then sewn together in rows (diagram 8b), which can be horizontal, vertical or diagonal. The rows are then sewn into a block. Some blocks are divided into quarters or halves, in which case the long seams will be sewn last.

8a

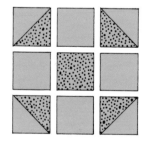

8b

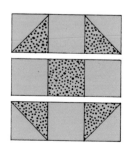

Other blocks do not fall into either of these categories. With the "Indiana Puzzle" block, for example, you start at the centre and work outwards. Whereas the "Bouquet" block has set-in patches, i.e. it has angled seam lines (see page 9). Sew a set-in patch in sections. Pin up to the point at which the seam changes direction and stitch to that point. Readjust the fabric, pin and stitch to the end of the seam line.

For either method, it is important that where seams meet, they meet precisely. Points should be pointed and not lopped off at the end. To achieve perfect results it helps to pin carefully any points you are trying to match up. You may have to ease or stretch some edges to fit. However, the most important consideration is to enjoy what you are doing and do it your way. I encourage all my students to work to the standard that suits each one of them best. The perfectionist will do it over and over again until it is just right; another person will happily overlook the staggered seams and imperfect stitching because she or he is completely caught up in the enthusiasm of the creative process. If you are enjoying yourself, you will probably go on to do more patchwork, and improvement comes with practice.

Choose a thread colour that will blend with all your patches, making sure that whatever you choose does not show through the lightest fabrics. For hand stitching by either method, use a 12–15 in/30–40 cm length of thread. To reduce tangling, use the thread as it comes off the reel; in other words, thread the needle with the loose end and put a knot in the end you cut.

For machine stitching, only the American method can be used (see page 101). There is also a convenient way of using the presser foot of the machine to measure the seam allowance, which is described in the "Spiderwebs and Cobwebs" workshop on page 76.

Pressing

For the American method, press the seams after each new patch is joined. The general rule is to press the seam toward the darker fabric, so that it will not show through on the right side. However, this is only a guideline, not an invariable rule. There are other points to be taken into consideration. For example, where multiple seams meet, press them in different directions if possible, so as to reduce the bulk. Try to avoid pressing a seam allowance under a planned quilting line, as this will add extra layers to quilt through.

Piece all the blocks together first before joining them together to make the quilt. When you have made up a number of blocks, lay them out in the proposed design on a bed or the floor. You may find that by shifting the actual-size blocks around, you find a more pleasing arrangement. Once the blocks are stitched together, you can also add a border (see below).

Piecing Appliqué

It may help to mark the background block as a guide to the accurate placing of the patches. For a simple block, finger press the background square into halves or quarters or diagonally and mark corresponding lines onto the original design. For more complicated blocks, you may need to *lightly* trace guidelines or reference points onto the background fabric. Make sure that these marks are either removable or will be hidden by the patches in the finished block.

If a patch has an inward (concave) curve, you can snip into the turning to make the curve lie smoothly when it is turned under (see diagram 9). Clip to within just a few threads of the marked line and no farther. Do not clip outward (convex) curves.

9

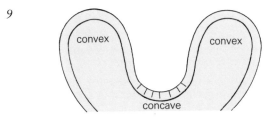

Start with any patch that will be partially covered by another. Continue in this way, building up layers. Use a 12–15 in/30–40 cm length of thread which matches the colour of the patch, not the background. Baste the patches to the background square, or, if you wish to pin the patches, pin from the back, so that the thread will not catch on the pins. Bring the needle through from the back and just catch a few threads on the edge of the patch. Take the needle back down into the background fabric exactly opposite where it emerged, and bring it up again about 1/16 in/2 mm farther along. Continue in this way, so that slanting stitches are formed on the back and the tiny stitches on the front are barely visible (see diagram 10).

10

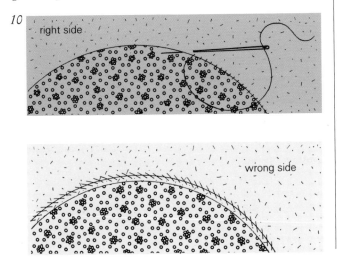

When the stitching is complete, trim the background fabric away from underneath the patches to reduce bulk, leaving only a single layer overall. To do this, cut the fabric 1/4 in/6 mm away from the stitching (see diagram 10). If you have been using paper templates, they can be removed at this point.

Where you have cut through seams, take a few stitches across the sewing lines to reinforce them. Appliquéd blocks can be set together in all the same ways as patchwork blocks: edge to edge, with alternating plain blocks, with sashing and on point.

Borders

Border strips can be added to surround or frame the patchwork or appliqué blocks. You can have a single or a double border and it can have either straight corners as described in the "Quick Quilts" workshop (page 23) or mitred corners as described in the "Cathedral Window" workshop (page 93). Instructions for the latter include wadding, which could be omitted at this stage.

Quilting

Mark the quilting pattern on your quilt top before you baste it to the wadding and backing.

Quilting Patterns

There are various sources for quilting patterns. You can use purchased stencils or trace patterns from books. Alternatively, it can be very rewarding to make your own quilting templates from cardboard or plastic, or you can follow tradition and use household objects, such as a wine glass, a saucer or a biscuit cutter, as templates. For simple straight lines of quilting, use a ruler or other straight edge.

There are two other methods of quilting which follow the patchwork designs. One is outline quilting, in which the stitching is worked 1/4 in/6 mm away from the seamlines of certain patches. You can use 1/4 in/6 mm wide masking tape to mark the distance or simply judge it by eye. The other method is called quilting "in-the-ditch" or "sink stitching", in which the stitches are made into or right next to the seamlines themselves and no additional marking is required.

If you are using a pattern which needs to be marked on the fabric, use the same marking tools as used for marking patches for cutting out. Always test them to be sure that they will not permanently mark the fabric. This is particularly important, as the patterns are marked on the right side of the fabric.

When choosing the backing fabric, take into consideration the colour of the quilting thread (see below). The backing fabric for your quilt should be about 2 in/5 cm larger on all sides than the quilt top. If you need to join the fabric, either seam the two lengths down the middle or split the second length and join it to either side of a middle panel (see diagram 11). If it makes more economical use of fabric, you might choose to have the seam going across the width. Press any seams open in order to reduce bulk.

11

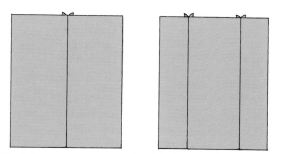

Wadding (see page 11) should also be about 2 in/5 cm larger all around than the quilt top. It comes in a variety of widths to suit most quilt sizes. However, if you need to join pieces, butt the edges; do not overlap them. Join them with herringbone stitch, pulling the thread just tight enough to hold the pieces together without bunching them (see diagram 12).

12

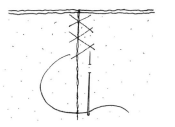

To prepare the quilt sandwich, lay the backing fabric right side down, preferably on a smooth surface. Tape the corners to hold the fabric down flat. Lay the wadding on top, taking care to smooth out any wrinkles. Lay the quilt top right side up centrally on top. Pin to hold the layers temporarily, then tack the three layers together in a grid, starting in the centre and working out to the edges. The rows of basting stitches should be 4–6 in/10–5 cm apart. Avoid the planned quilting lines. The important thing is to hold the three layers together securely and smoothly.

Quilting by Hand

To work the quilting patterns, choose the shortest looking betweens needle that you think you can manage. The shorter the needle, the smaller the stitch is the usual consensus. In the beginning, just use what is comfort-

able and don't worry about the size of your stitch. It is more important to have them even than incredibly tiny. If you have never used a thimble, take a deep breath and start today. Pushing a needle through several layers of fabric plus wadding will very quickly cause pain to an unprotected finger.

Choose your quilting thread in a colour to blend with the quilt top and you will see the contour lines of stitching. Choose a contrasting colour and you will see each stitch.

Cut a 15–18 in/40–50 cm length of thread. As in hand piecing, use a single strand of thread as it comes off the reel, with a knot in the end you cut. Insert the needle ½–¾ in/1–2 cm away from where you intend to begin. Bring it out at the starting point and pull on the thread until the knot pops through the backing fabric and lodges in the wadding. The quilting stitch is simply a running stitch through all three layers. The hand underneath feels the point of the needle as it comes through the backing and deflects it upward to form the stitch. The tension on the thread should create gentle contours, not gathers.

Start quilting in the centre of the quilt and work outward. Avoid quilting at random or you will end up with puckers and bumps in the quilt. The use of a quilting hoop will also help to give better results. You may want to protect the finger on the underneath hand with a second thimble or other covering. Some people prefer to build up a quilter's callus. Like everything to do with quilting, there are many possible solutions.

At the end of a length of thread, make your last stitch and bring the needle out to the top (see diagram 13a). Take a tiny backstitch through the top fabric only and bring the needle out again (diagram 13b). Make a single knot in the thread about ¼ in/6 mm from the backstitch. Re-insert the needle just through to the wadding (diagram 13c), and bring it out to the top again some distance away. Pull the thread until the knot pops into the wadding and lies buried inside it. Trim off the thread level with the quilt top (diagram 13d).

13a

13b

13c

13d

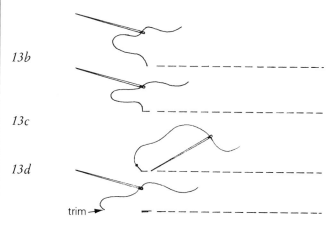

trim ➤

Quilting by Machine

This is successful only if you have a "walking" foot or similar attachment for your sewing machine, which will feed both the top and bottom layers evenly through the machine. Choose a very simple pattern of straight lines.

Pin-baste the three layers together, using safety pins about 6 in/15 cm apart in all directions. Avoid placing them on quilting lines. Place your machine on a large table, so that the quilt is supported at the side and the back while it is being stitched. Roll the quilt up tightly in order to fit the bulk under the arm of the sewing machine.

Finishing

When all the quilting is complete, bind the edges of the quilt with a double binding cut on the bias. To cut the binding, fold the chosen fabric at 45° to the grain line and cut strips using a rotary cutter and ruler. The strips should be six times the finished width of the binding. Join the strips to make the required length. Join them with a diagonal seam (see diagram 14) and press the

14

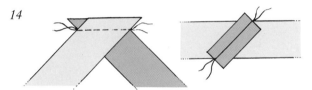

seams open. Fold the binding in half lengthwise and press carefully.

Place the binding so that the cut edges are towards the edges of the quilt. Try to avoid having a seam in the binding falling at a corner or in the centre of the sides, where constant folding will weaken it. Begin at one corner and leave a generous amount of binding for the final join. Pin the binding in position until the first corner is reached. Fold the binding up vertically at a 45° angle (see diagram 15a), finger press the fold and pin along the fold (diagram 15b). Stitch through all layers (the finished width of the binding away from the edge) finishing the stitches exactly on the fold line. Fasten off.

15a   *15b*

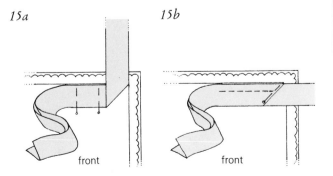

Fold the binding back over itself, so that it now runs parallel to the second edge of the quilt. Pin up to the next corner. Crease and pin as before. Stitch right from the edge of the first side up to the second corner crease and fasten off (diagram 15c). Repeat until the last corner has been mitred.

15c

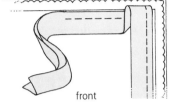

To join the binding, carefully measure the two ends so that they meet exactly. Add an extra ¼ in/6 mm to each end for seam allowance, then cut the ends diagonally in the same direction. Join the ends with a diagonal seam. Pin the remaining binding in position (diagram 15d) and sew from the last corner until you reach the starting point of the stitching.

15d

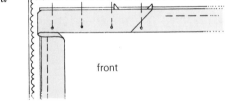

Trim the surplus wadding and backing. Fold the binding over to the back of the quilt to align with the line of stitching. Hem in position, folding the corners as shown in diagram 16 to complete the mitres. Hem the back of the mitre but do not stitch it down at the front of the quilt.

16

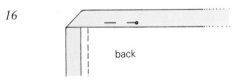

Finally, after all your hard work, please embroider your name and a date on your quilt. All artists should sign their work!

Quick Quilts
using the Rotary Cutter and the Sewing Machine

Pam Lintott

Pam Lintott's interest in patchwork dates back to the late 1960s and early 70s; she was living in the United States and discovered American quilts. Subsequent travels around the world, fuelled her interest. Then she and her husband opened a bookshop in Dorking, Surrey; above the shop was a splendid beam-ceilinged room "just waiting to be draped with quilts". And so, in 1981, The Quilt Room was born.

&

Rosemary Miller

Rosemary Miller began working at The Quilt Room in 1983, and became a partner the following year. Like Pam, she is a busy wife and mother as well as a businesswoman. Her own interest in patchwork was first stimulated by a beautiful antique Log Cabin quilt; and she continues to enjoy expressing her love of fabrics in her quiltmaking.

Sources and Approaches

Owning one's own quilting shop has some very obvious advantages. There are always ideas being discussed, new methods to try and, most important of all, lots of fabrics to give one inspiration. The great disadvantage, though, is that running the shop leaves little time in which to put all those ideas into practice. This was the reason we both became so interested in quick piecing methods. Suddenly, with the advent of the rotary cutter, it became possible to cut and piece quilts in hours – even possibly finish them in a day.

It is no exaggeration to say that the rotary cutter has revolutionized patchwork. Its true potential took some time to be realized, but now it means that all those quilts we all mean to "get round to one day" have a better chance of becoming a reality!

The essence of the revolution is a totally new approach to the piecing of fabric – often sewing, then cutting, rather than the other way round. There is no need for templates and no need for marking sewing and cutting lines on your fabric. It certainly seems too good to be true, but it really works. Accuracy is of the utmost importance, though, and care must be taken in checking measurements before cutting.

Snowball with Nine Patch
(previous page)

Snowball blocks alternate with Nine Patch in this cotton bed quilt. Instructions for making it are given on page 29. The quilt in the photograph is pieced by machine and hand quilted.

66 × 90 in/168 × 229 cm

Quick Quilts – Techniques and Projects

In this workshop we aim to teach quick piecing techniques using the rotary cutter and sewing machine. We guide you through making several quilts using various techniques but this is only the beginning. Once you have grasped the idea of quick piecing there is no end to what you can do.

It is important to read through the general section on techniques before commencing any of the quilts.

Equipment
Rotary cutter
Cutting mat at least 18 × 24 in/45 × 60 cm
Quilting ruler 24 × 6 in marked in eighths of an inch (or similar metric rule)
Trudie Hughes "Rotary Mate" (see page 30)
A 12 in/30 cm quilter's right-angled triangle, or quilter's 12½ in/31 cm square
Sewing machine

Machine Stitching
It is vital to maintain a consistent seam allowance of a SCANT ¼ in/6 mm. *This allowance has been included in all of the measurements in this workshop.* Position the fabric so that the edge of the presser foot is aligned with the edge of the fabric as described in the "Spiderwebs and Cobwebs" Workshop, see page 76.

Set the machine for 12–15 stitches per inch/5–6 per centimetre with even tension, using a size 80/12 needle.

Chain piecing is the technique of feeding pieces through the sewing machine without lifting the presser foot and without cutting the thread. Always chain piece when you can – it saves time and thread.

Chain Piecing Blocks
1 Referring to the sample block (see diagram 1), place A and B of row 1 together with right sides facing, making sure the corners are in line.

1

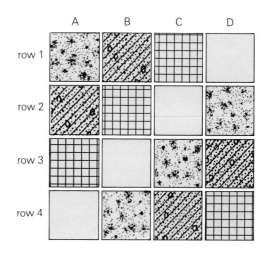

2 Stitch, but leave the presser foot down and do not cut thread.

3 Continue sewing A and B of rows 2, 3 and 4, without lifting the presser foot, thus keeping the squares linked together. Continue until all A and B squares for that block are joined.

4 Join the C squares to the AB squares in the same way.

5 Continue in this way until all the squares are linked together (see diagram 2). It is not necessary to cut the threads.

2

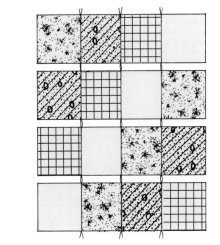

6 With right sides together match seams and sew horizontal rows together. Press.

Pressing is of paramount importance at every stage. Always try to press pairs of squares or triangles so that one set of seam allowances goes one way and the other set goes the opposite way. This creates less bulk. However, seams should be pressed towards the darker fabric where possible. When pressing a set of strips, place strips across the ironing board with the seam allowances right side up and darker strip on the left. Holding the fabric with left hand, iron from the right, pressing the seams towards the left. Turn the strips over and press on the right side of fabric in the same manner.

Using a Rotary Cutter

1 To straighten the fabric, fold the fabric in half, selvedge to selvedge, then fold again, making sure that the folded edge and selvedges are aligned. Place the ruler across the fabric so that one of the perpendicular lines marked on it is aligned with the double fold of the fabric. Hold the ruler firmly with your left hand and the cutter in the right. Keeping the blade against the edge of the ruler, push the cutter away from the body in one even movement (see diagram 3a). Left-handed people should reverse these instructions but the important thing is to cut away from the body.

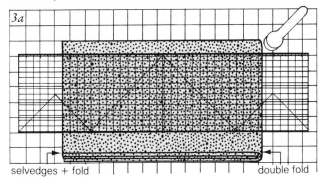

selvedges + fold / double fold

2 Rotate the cutting mat so that the ruler can still be held firmly with the left hand, and you are now ready to cut strips, moving from left to right across the fabric (see diagram 3b).

3b

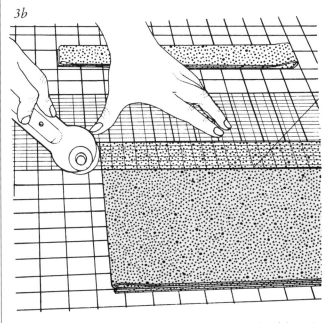

Note: Check every 18 in/45 cm or so that the fabric is still straight by opening up a strip. If the cuts are not perpendicular to the fold, the strips, when opened, will form a shallow zigzag, and you will need to re-straighten the edge.

Cutting Strips

Note: All of the quilts in our workshop start by cutting strips across the width of the fabric.

To cut a 2 in/5 cm wide strip, for example, position the 2 in/5 cm line marked on the ruler on the cut edge of the fabric and one of the perpendicular lines on the double fold; then cut. Remember, a 2 in/5 cm cut strip will end up measuring 1½ in/3.8 cm when finished.

Cutting Squares and Rectangles

1 Cut a strip of the width required (finished) plus ½ in/1.2 cm for seam allowances. Leave it folded.

2 Trim off the selvedge/fold edge. Working across from this cut edge, cut the strips into the desired size of square or rectangle, adding ½ in/1.2 cm seam allowance. Depending on the size of square or rectangle, it is sometimes necessary to unfold the double-fold edge to obtain 2 extra squares or rectangles.

Piecing Four-Patch

1 Join 2 strips of contrasting fabric; press the seam towards the darker side. Repeat with 2 identical strips (see diagram 4a).

4a

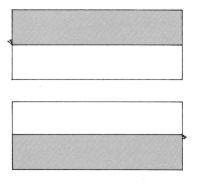

2 Place one joined strip on the other with right sides together reversing colours. The seams will butt together (see diagram 4b).

4b

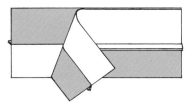

3 Using the rotary cutter and ruler, trim the selvedges. Cut strips of the required width through the double thickness. Leave them in pairs (see diagram 4c).

4c

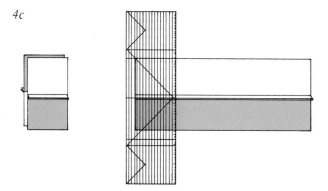

4 Chain piece the squares together (see diagram 4d).

4d

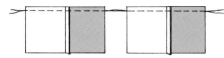

5 Cut the threads and press the square open (see diagram 4e).

4e

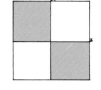

Piecing Nine-Patch

1 A Nine-Patch block has 3 sets of strips, rows 1 and 3 being the same. Make a set of strips for each row. Press the seams towards the darker fabric.

2 Place rows 1 and 2 together with right sides facing, and butting seams (see diagram 5a). Cut them to the required size. Chain piece them together matching seams (see diagram 5b).

5a   *5b*

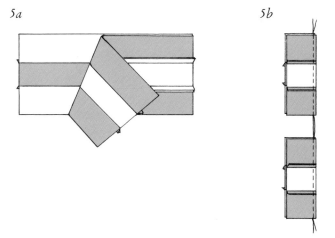

3 Cut row 3 to the required size and add to row 2 (see diagrams 5c and 5d).

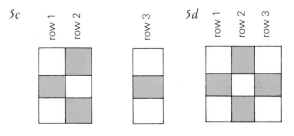

Cutting Half-Square Triangles

These triangles occupy half a square and are measured on the two shorter sides, the long edge being on the bias. They are formed from a square cut $7/8$ in/2.2 cm larger than the desired finished size of the square; for example, if the finished size is 4 in/10 cm, cut a square measuring $4\,7/8$ in/12.2 cm, then cut this in half diagonally.

Alternative Quick Piecing Method

1 Take 2 contrasting fabric strips and open them to full width. Lay fabric A right side up on the cutting mat. Lay fabric B wrong side up on top of fabric A, matching the cut edges. Bring fabric B back on itself and then fabric A on top, taking care to match the cut edges (see diagram 6a).

6a

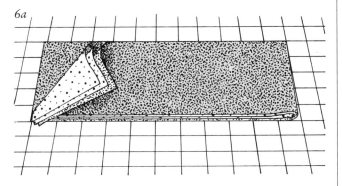

2 Cut these strips into squares. Cut each square diagonally in half (see diagram 6b). Stack the triangles on top of each other. The pairs of triangles to be sewn together are now conveniently placed with right sides facing, ready to be chain-pieced along the diagonal edge (see diagram 6c).

6b

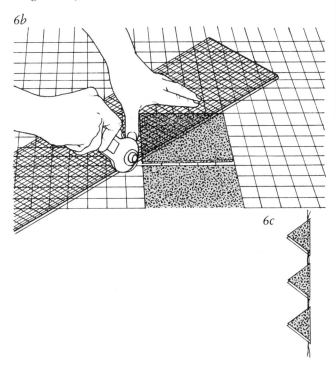

6c

3 Cut the thread between pairs and snip the corners of the triangle (see diagram 6d). Press the square open (see diagram 6e).

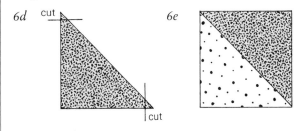

6d cut cut *6e*

Adding Borders

We have kept all our borders extremely simple, limiting them to one or two borders with straight corners. Pieced or strip borders and mitred corners (see page 93) will all add to the individual look of your quilt.

The cutting instructions for the borders and binding state the number of strips to be cut. These are cut across the width of the fabric and joined to make one continuous strip, which is then cut to the required lengths to fit that quilt. If you prefer not to have any seams in your borders you must adjust the fabric requirement, which will be the length of your quilt; that is, the border strips will be cut lengthwise, with the longest strips determining the fabric amount.

Straight Corners

The borders are joined in the order shown in diagram 7. Begin by measuring the two lengthwise sides of the quilt. Opposite borders *must* be the same length. If the sides are not quite equal, cut the border strip the exact length of the *shorter* side. Mark the halves and quarters of both quilt and border with pins. Placing right sides together and matching the pins, stitch quilt and border together, easing the longer side to fit where necessary. Repeat on the opposite side.

7

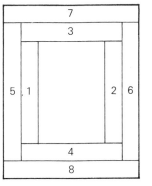

Measure the other two sides, including the borders, and add these borders in the same manner. Add the second border, if any, in the same order as before.

Finishing the Quilt

Once the borders have been added you are ready to layer your pieced top, wadding and backing together (see page 16). The backing fabric will normally need to be seamed in order to make a piece of the required size. Quilt either by hand or by machine. If you are machine quilting, safety pins are a good, speedy alternative to tacking. A walking foot is a must when machine quilting (see page 17); if you are considering a new machine at any stage, make sure that it can take a walking foot.

For binding the edges we recommend a double binding; see the instructions for this on page 17. Note, however, that our bindings are not cut on the bias. Measurements for the width of the binding strips are given with each quilt.

Rail Fence

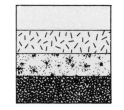

8a

This simple but effective block (see diagram 8a) is a good one for your first Quick Quilt, as the three seams in each square will soon reveal whether or not you are maintaining a scant ¼ in/6 mm seam allowance. Machine quilting has been worked "in-the-ditch" around each square.

The quilt shown is for a single bed but we have also provided fabric quantities for a double bed quilt.

	Single	Double
Size:	62 × 92 in/	92 × 92 in/
	158 × 234 cm	234 × 234 cm
Block size:	6 in/15 cm	6 in/15 cm
No. of blocks:	9 × 14 blocks	14 × 14 blocks

Fabric Requirements

Note: All fabrics are 45 in/115 cm wide and strips are cut across the width of the fabric.

For patchwork:	1⅜ yards/1.30 m each of four different fabrics ranging in tone from light to dark (Double: 2 yards/1.80 m)
For border:	1⅛ yards/1 m (Double: 1¼ yards/1.10 m)
For binding:	⅝ yard/60 cm (Double: same amount)
For backing:	5¼ yards/4.80 m (Double: same amount)
Wadding:	65 × 95 in/165 × 242 cm (Double: 95 × 95 in/242 × 242 cm)

Cutting Instructions

For patchwork:	22 × 2 in/5 cm strips of each fabric (Double: 33 × 2 in/5 cm strips of each fabric)
For border:	8 × 4½ in/11.5 cm strips (Double: 9 × 4½ in/11.5 cm strips)
For binding:	8 × 2 in/5 cm strips (Double: 9 × 2 in/5 cm strips)

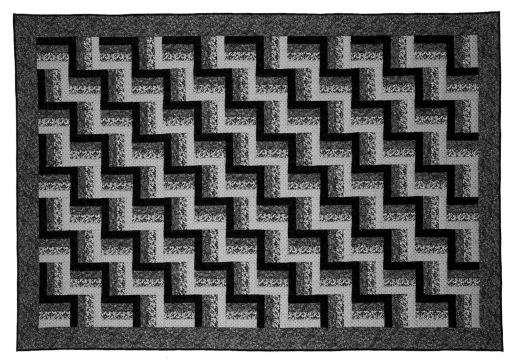

Method

1 Join the four strips together; press seams towards the darker fabric.

2 Check the width of the joined strips. If your seam allowance is correct, the strips should measure 6½ in/ 16.5 cm, and you can proceed to cut squares from the strips (see diagram 8b). If your measurement is different, cut the squares to that size.

8b

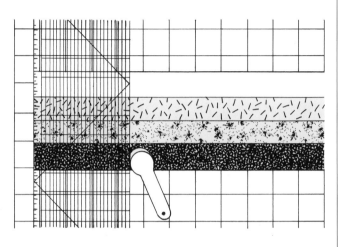

3 To create the Rail Fence pattern arrange the vertical blocks with the dark strip on the left and the horizontal blocks with the dark strip on the bottom (see diagram 8c). Chain piece the blocks together (see diagram 8d).

8c   *8d*

6½ in/16.5 cm   6½ in/16.5 cm

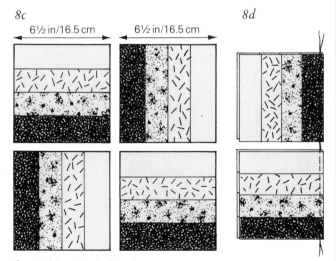

4 Add a single border.

Finishing the Quilt

5 Prepare the wadding and backing as required, and assemble the three layers (see page 16). Quilt and bind as desired.

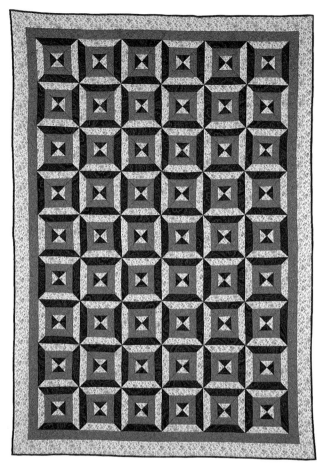

Mitred Square

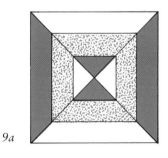

9a

Like Rail Fence, this block (see diagram 9a) involves joining strips, but here the bands of strips are cut into triangles, which are then joined to form squares. The blocks on this quilt have been machine quilted "in-the-ditch".

The quilt shown is for a single bed but we have also provided fabric quantities for a double bed quilt.

	Single	Double
Size:	64 × 91 in/	91 × 91 in/
	163 × 231 cm	231 × 231 cm
Block size:	9 in/23 cm	9 in/23 cm
No. of blocks:	6 × 9 blocks	9 × 9 blocks

Fabric Requirements

Note: All fabrics are 45 in/115 cm and strips are cut across the width of the fabric.

For patchwork:	1⅞ yards/1.80 m (Double: 2¾ yards/ 2.60 m) each of three fabrics – light, medium and dark
For border 1:	⅝ yard/60 cm (Double: ¾ yard/ 70 cm)
For border 2:	⅞ yard/80 cm (Double: 1 yard/ 90 cm)
For binding:	⅝ yard/60 cm (Double: same amount)
For backing:	5¼ yards/4.80 m (Double: same amount
Wadding:	67 × 94 in/170 × 240 cm (Double: 94 in/240 cm square)

Cutting Instructions

For patchwork:	32 × 2 in/5 cm strips of each fabric (Double: 48 × 2 in/5 cm strips of each fabric)
For border 1:	7 × 2½ in/6.3 cm strips (Double: 8 × 2½ in/6.3 cm strips)
For border 2:	8 × 3½ in/9 cm strips (Double: 9 × 3½ in/9 cm strips)
For binding:	8 × 2 in/5 cm strips (Double: 9 × 2 in/5 cm strips)

Method

1 Join 3 strips together and press the seams towards darker fabric.

2 Lay one set of strips on the cutting mat, right side up, and place another set of strips on top, right side down, reversing colours and butting seams.

3 Using a large right-angled triangle (or a large quilting square), cut triangles as illustrated, making sure that the tip of the triangle just touches the top cut edge and that the lines of the triangle are parallel with the bottom cut edge (see diagram 9b). You should get 7 triangles to each strip. Handle the triangles with care, as they have two bias edges.

9b

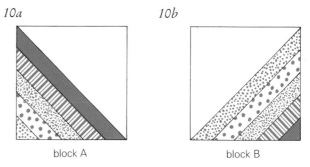

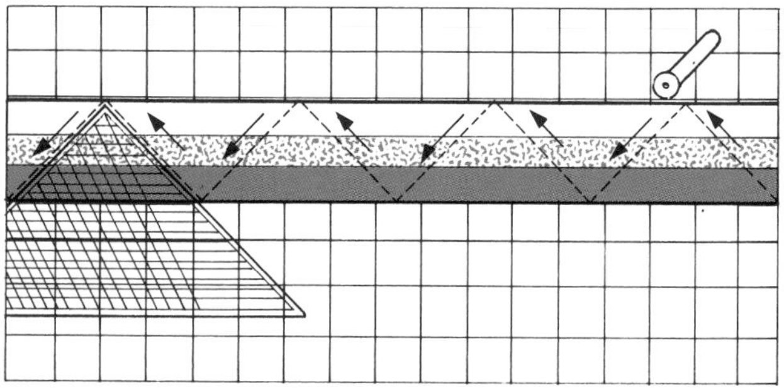

4 Chain piece the triangles together in pairs, and then form them into squares (see diagram 9c).

9c

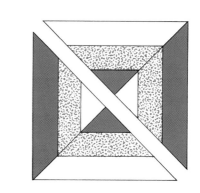

5 Chain piece the blocks together. Add a double border.

Finishing the Quilt

6 Prepare the wadding and backing as required, and assemble the three layers (see page 16). Quilt and bind as desired.

Roman Stripe

10a   *10b*

block A   block B

A rich, bold colour scheme featuring dark purple and turquoise enhances the strong, classic lines of Roman Stripe (which has the advantage of being very quick to piece), see block diagrams 10a and 10b. The diagonal lines of quilting are carried across the whole block.

Size (single):	62 × 90 in/158 × 229 cm
Block size:	7 in/18 cm
No. of blocks	8 × 12 blocks

Fabric Requirements

Note: All fabrics are 45 in/115 cm wide and strips are cut across the width of the fabric.

For patchwork:	⅞ yard/80 cm each of five fabrics *or* 80 × 1½ in/3.8 cm strips of different fabrics for a scrap effect 2¾ yards/2.50 m background fabric

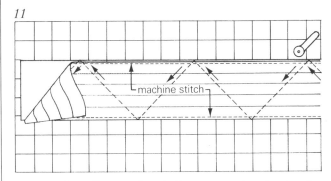

For border: ⅞ yard/80 cm
For binding: ⅝ yard/60 cm
For backing: 5¼ yards/4.80 m
Wadding: 65 × 93 in/165 × 236 cm

Cutting Instructions
For patchwork: 16 × 1½ in/3.8 cm strips of each of five fabrics.
Background fabric: 16 × 5½ in/14 cm strips BUT do not cut this until you have checked the measurement of your sewn strips
For border: 8 × 3½ in/9 cm strips
For binding: 8 × 2 in/5 cm strips

Method
1 Take 1 strip of each of the 5 fabrics and join together so that the colour sequence graduates from light to dark. Repeat until you have formed 16 strip units. Press.

2 Measure the pieced strip unit – it should be 5½ in/14 cm. Cut the background fabric into 16 × 5½ in/14 cm strips (or the exact width of your particular strip).

3 Lay pieced strip unit and background strip, right sides together, matching cut edges. Pin and machine stitch along both long edges.

4 Using the large right-angled triangle (or quilting square), cut triangles as shown in diagram 11, making sure that the tip of the triangle touches the top cut edge and that the lines of the triangle are parallel with the bottom cut edge. You should get 6 triangles to each strip unit. Handle them with care as they have two bias edges.

5 Gently pull apart the stitches at top of each triangle. Open out and press the seams towards the background fabric. You will have 48 blocks of Block A and 48 blocks of Block B (see diagrams 10a and 10b).

6 Trim the points, then chain piece the blocks together alternating Blocks A and B.

7 Add a single border.

Finishing the Quilt
8 Prepare the wadding and backing as required, and assemble the three layers (see page 16). Quilt and bind as desired.

Milky Way

12

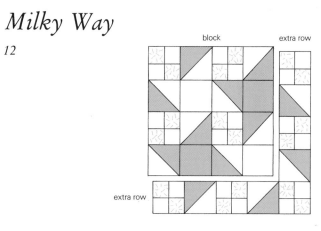

This effective quilt is made up of three basic units – a square, a four-patch and quick pieced half-square triangles (see diagram 12). Machine quilting has been worked around the stars "in-the-ditch".

Size (double):	92 in square/234 cm square
Block size:	16 in/40.5 cm
No. of blocks:	5 × 5 blocks plus an extra strip on two sides to complete the design

Fabric Requirements
Note: All fabrics are 45 in/115 cm and strips are cut across the width of the fabric.

For patchwork:	Fabric A (light): 4 yards/3.70 m
	Fabric B (dark): 2⅞ yards/2.70 m
	Fabric C (medium): 1¼ yards/1.20 m
For border:	1¼ yards/1.10 m
For binding:	⅝ yard/60 cm
For backing:	5¼ yards/4.80 m
Wadding:	95 × 95 in/242 × 242 cm

Cutting Instructions
For patchwork:

Fabric A:	16 × 2½ in/6.3 cm strips (to form Four-Patch)
	6 × 4½ in/11.5 cm strips. Then cut these into 50 × 4½ in/11.5 cm squares
	14 × 4⅞ in/12.2 cm strips (to form 220 Half Triangles)
Fabric B:	6 × 4½ in/11.5 cm strips. Then cut these into 50 × 4½ in/11.5 cm squares
	14 × 4⅞ in/12.2 cm strips (to form 220 Half Triangles)
Fabric C:	16 × 2½ in/6.3 cm strips (to form Four-Patch)
For border:	9 × 4½ in/11.5 cm strips
For binding:	9 × 2 in/5 cm strips

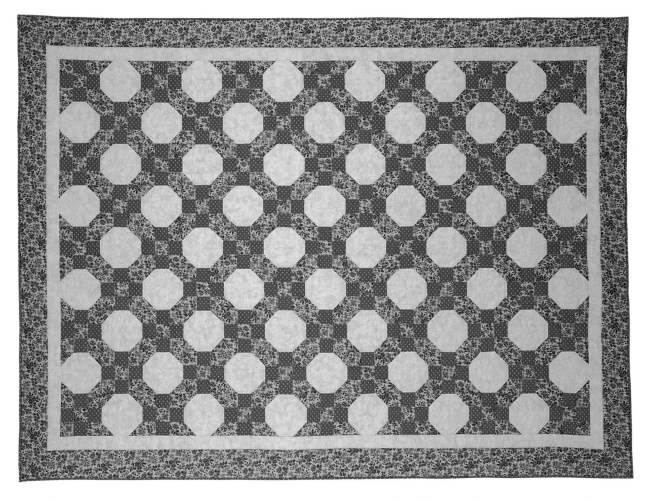

Method

1 Form 121 Four-Patch squares using fabrics A and C.

2 Using the Half-Square Triangle Quick Piecing Method described on page 23, form 220 squares from fabrics A and B.

3 Referring to the Milky Way block, i.e. the arrangement of 4 × 4 squares without the extra row (see diagram 12), chain piece the squares into twenty-five blocks.

4 Chain piece the blocks together to form 5 strips of 5 blocks. To complete the design, add an extra row to the right hand side of the quilt identical to the left hand side. Add an extra row to the bottom of the quilt identical to the top.

5 Add a single border.

Finishing the Quilt

6 Prepare the wadding and backing as required, and assemble the three layers (see page 16). Quilt and bind as desired.

Snowball with Nine Patch

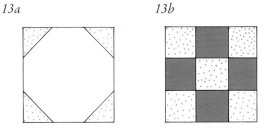

13a   *13b*

This quilt is made up of two alternating blocks – the Snowball and the Nine-Patch. The Snowball is a square whose corners have been cut off and replaced by triangles (see diagram 13a), and it combines very effectively with the Nine-Patch block (see diagram 13b).

Size (single):   66 × 90 in/168 × 229 cm
Block size: 6 in/15 cm
No. of blocks: 9 × 13 blocks

Fabric Requirements
Note: All fabrics are 45 in/115 cm wide and strips are cut across the width of the fabric.

For patchwork: Fabric A (light): 2 yards/1.80 m
Fabric B (medium): 2⅜ yards/2.20 m
Fabric C (dark): 1¼ yards/1.20 m
For border 1: ⅝ yard/60 cm
For border 2: 1⅛ yard/1 m
For binding: ⅝ yard/60 cm
For backing: 5¼ yards/4.80 m
Wadding: 69 × 93 in/175 × 236 cm

Cutting Instructions

For patchwork: Fabric A: 10 × 6½ in/16.5 cm strips (then cut these into 58 × 6½ in/16.5 cm squares)
Fabric B: 20 × 2½ in/6.3 cm strips (to form Nine-Patch);
9 × 2⅞ in/7.3 cm strips (to form triangles for Snowball block)
Fabric C: 16 × 2½ in/6.3 cm strips (to form Nine-Patch)
For border 1: 7 × 2½ in/6.3 cm strips
For border 2: 8 × 4½ in/11.5 cm strips
For binding: 8 × 2 in/5 cm strips

Method

1 Make 59 Nine-Patch blocks using fabrics B and C.

2 Trudie Hughes has come up with the best method of creating the Snowball block. Her "Rotary Mate" (a clear plastic ruler) has marked on it "Speedy Triangles" (right-angled triangles in various sizes) for cutting off the corners of the block. Using the 2 in "Speedy Triangle", cut off all corners from each 6½ in/16.5 cm fabric A square (see diagram 14).

14

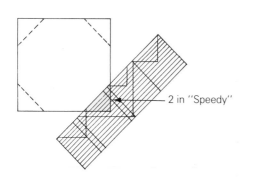

2 in "Speedy"

3 Taking the 2⅞ in/7.3 cm strips of fabric B, cut these into 2⅞ in/7.3 cm squares, then cut the squares in half diagonally forming 232 right-angled triangles. The points of these triangles need to be trimmed off to ensure a perfect fit to the Snowball block. This can be done easily by stacking the triangles and placing the ruler on the 2½ in/6.3 cm lines as shown in diagram 15.

15

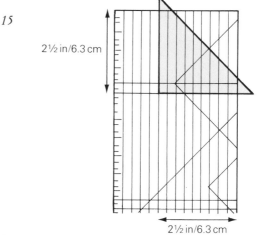

2½ in/6.3 cm

2½ in/6.3 cm

4 Piece the fabric B triangles to all four corners of the fabric A Snowball pieces. Press the seams towards the triangles.

5 Join the blocks, alternating the Snowball blocks with the Nine-Patch blocks, pinning the point where the Snowball triangle joins the Nine-Patch to ensure a perfect match.

6 Add a double border.

Finishing the Quilt

7 Prepare the wadding and backing as required, and assemble the three layers (see page 16). Quilt and bind as desired.

Melon Patch

16

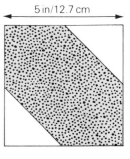

5 in/12.7 cm

The next two quilts are extremely effective and very cleverly pieced in that the cut-off triangles from one quilt are trimmed and used in the second. Instructions are given in detail below for Melon Patch. For Reverse Melon Patch the same number of blocks is used but the units are smaller.

Size (lap quilt): 43 × 63 in/119 × 160 cm
Block size: 5 in/12.7 cm
No. of blocks: 7 × 11 blocks

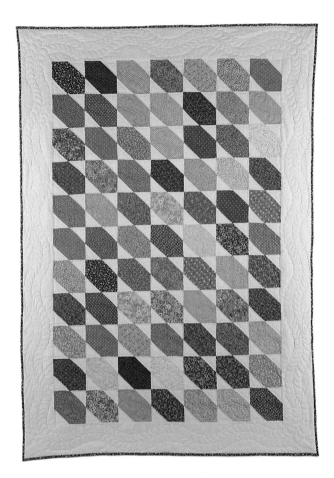

Fabric Requirements

Note: All fabrics are 45 in/115 cm wide and strips are cut across the width of the fabric.

For patchwork: Scrap prints: 77 × at least 5½ in/ 14 cm square
                Calico: ⅞ yard/80 cm
For border: 1 yard/90 cm
For binding: ½ yard/40 cm
For backing: 1⅞ yards/170 cm
Wadding: 46 × 66 in/116 × 167 cm

Cutting Instructions

For patchwork: Cut 77 × 5½ in/14 cm squares from print fabrics
                Cut 7 × 3⅜ in/8.6 cm strips from the calico.
For border: Cut 6 × 5½ in/14 cm strips
For binding: Cut 6 × 2 in/5 cm strips

Method

1 Using the 2½ in "Speedy Triangle" on the Trudie Hughes "Rotary Mate", cut off two opposite corners from the 5½ in/14 cm print fabric squares. Save these cut-off triangles.

2 Cut the calico strips into 3⅜ in/8.6 cm squares and cut in half diagonally forming 154 right-angled triangles. The points of these triangles need to be trimmed off to ensure a perfect fit to the Melon Patch block (see diagram 16). This can be done easily by stacking the triangles and placing the ruler on the 3 in/7.6 cm lines as described and illustrated for the previous quilt.

3 Referring to diagram 16, piece the calico triangles to the print fabric to form the Melon Patch block, then press the seams towards the triangles. Join all the blocks together and add a single border (see page 23).

Finishing the Quilt

4 Prepare the wadding and backing as required, and assemble the three layers (see page 16). Quilt and bind as desired.

Reverse Melon Patch

Using the 1½ in "Speedy Triangle" on the Trudie Hughes "Rotary Mate", cut off two opposite corners from each of 77 × 3½ in/9 cm calico squares. Next place the ¼ in/6 mm line of ruler diagonally from point to point and trim surplus fabric from the cut-off triangles. Piece and join blocks as above. Add a single border. Bind and quilt as desired.

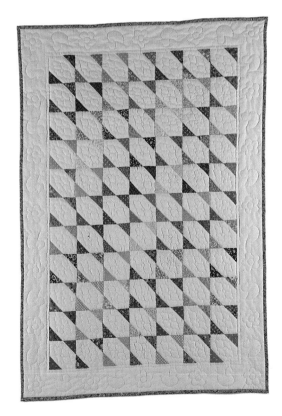

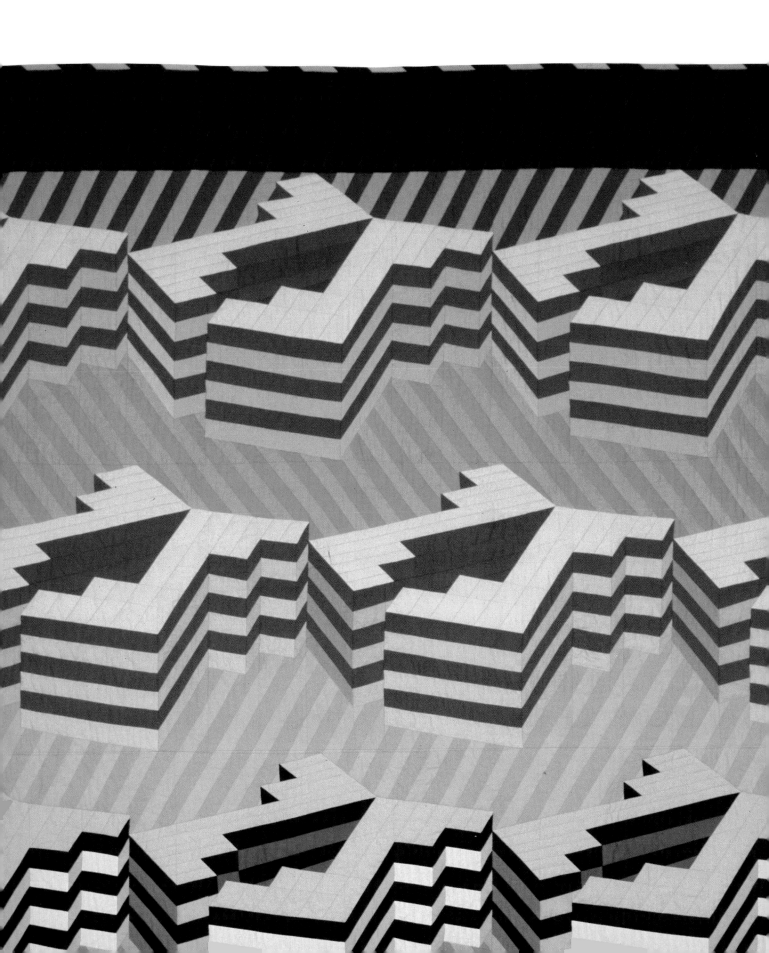

Paper and Fabric Collage

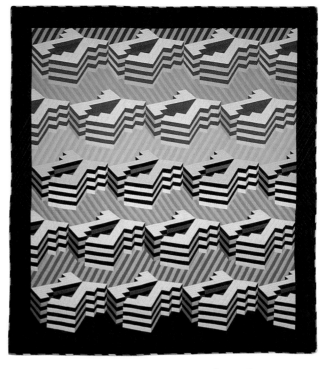

Pauline Burbid<u>ge</u>

After studying fashion and textiles at St Martin's School of Art, London, Pauline Burbidge began, in 1975, to make quilts. Her growing passion for patchwork and quiltmaking led her to produce unique works of art. Her international reputation has grown through solo and mixed exhibitions in Britain and abroad. Her quilts have been purchased by major art collections. Since 1979 she has taught quiltmaking and design classes throughout Britain, as well as in Australia, the United States and Germany.

Sources and Approaches

My work has grown from the love of the traditional craft. The thing that inspired me to make quilts in the first place was simply looking at old quilts and books on quiltmaking. I particularly admire quilts made around 1900–20, especially the Amish quilts. I also like the rough-and-ready farm quilts, often made in a very simple technique, with squares or rectangles pieced together in a balanced but asymmetrical way.

From the outset, pieced quilts held more appeal for me than appliqué ones, because of the design quality that this technique naturally produced. The scale of the quilts excited me, together with the bold patterns created by repeated blocks.

After initially making two traditional-style quilts, I began my own designing. The use of pattern – such as stripes – in my choice of subject, together with that formed by the repeated unit, play a significant role in my finished designs. I tend to work through chosen design themes. My work so far divides into three main phases: pictorial/figurative imagery, from 1976 to 1980, three-dimensional illusion works, from 1980 to 1986, and works based on torn paper collage studies from 1986 to the present. In this latter category I have worked mainly on still-life and landscape subjects.

My pictorial quilts were based mainly on animals, birds and butterflies, often set in rows of repeating blocks. I also worked on a series based on Egyptian art, which was initiated by a commission on this subject. I loved the imagery, but even more inspirational was the colouring of these ancient objects, especially the mummy cases. At this stage I began to dye my own fabric in order to achieve a better colour range.

The 3D illusion works were based on the theme of flat geometric pattern, which I used to create an illusion of depth. Mastering the geometry of the shapes entailed developing my technical drawing skills. The experiment with colour continued, and it became obvious that I had to be much more aware of tonal value.

My current work, based around paper collage as a starting point, is illustrated in this workshop. I have chosen this medium in a deliberate effort to liberate my image making; it forces me to be bold and to dispense with fussy detail. Another advantage is that I am working not with line but with areas of colour, which can naturally be interpreted in fabric. At the moment I am either setting up still-life objects or working from photographs (my own or other people's).

I am currently completing a series on fish images, trying to portray a feeling of movement and water refraction in these; this also allows me to abstract the image. I continue to work with repeated blocks, but choose not to use identical images in them, but rather make them change and grow throughout the quilt (as in "Joining Forces"). My palette continues to be bold, juxtaposing bright colour with black, white and greys.

Many traditional patchwork and quilting techniques use hand stitching exclusively. Although I love the texture of hand quilting, I have always preferred to use the sewing machine and enjoy the flexibility and

Liquorice Allsorts
(previous page)

The design for this quilt was based on the same step models as "Mirrored Steps". The title "Liquorice Allsorts" occurred to me only after completing the quilt, as the colours and strips reminded me of these popular English sweets.

I dyed almost all of the fabric for this quilt and used a large colour range, from vibrant primaries on the lower edge to much more subtle pastels at the top of the quilt.

The whole quilt is pieced and quilted by machine, using both sink-stitching and topstitching.

88 × 95 in/224 × 242 cm

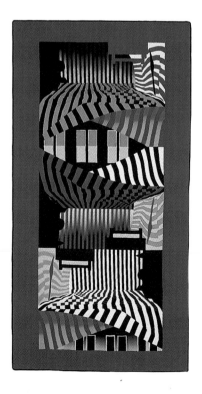

**Striped Canopy and
Canopy II**

*These quilts were commissioned
by Nottingham County Council
for the foyer of the Mansfield Arts
Centre. The designs were based
on the Mansfield Market Square,
where striped canopies hang over
the fruit and vegetable stalls,
acting as weather shields.*

*I have used dip-dyed fabric for
the first time in "Canopy II"
(below left).*

121 × 95 in/307 × 242 cm
(Striped Canopy)
50 × 97 in/127 × 246 cm
(Canopy II)

quality that can be achieved on modern machines, as well as the way they speed up the labour involved in quiltmaking.

My early experience of garment making helped me perfect my technique of machine piecing fairly quickly . The machine technique lends itself especially well to hard-edged geometric-type shapes, and thus influenced the design. I enjoyed working within these limitations; however, when I began to work with paper collage, I realized that my technique would have to change, so I introduced fabric appliqué and machine embroidery to accommodate these new, freer forms.

I prefer to quilt as well as piece by machine. For the first six years I quilted by "sink-stitching" through the seams of the pieced work into the wadding and backing fabric, aiming to hide the quilting stitches in the seamlines. In later 3D work I deliberately used decorative top-stitching for my quilting in order to add more depth to the image.

Since 1986 I have used a multi-needle quilting machine, which I hire in a local factory. I have had a lot to learn about operating these huge machines, and have had some disasters along the way. Generally,

however, it has speeded up my production, leaving me free to spend more time on the design and assembling of the top cloth. The machines are limited to an overall repeating pattern.

The fabrics I use are mainly solid colours; I like the bold quality that this produces. I use mainly pure cotton, plain-weave, dress-weight fabric. Some of it I dye myself, to obtain a good, wide colour range. Occasionally I have made quilts from Honan silk, which I have found the best-quality silk for piecing. Recently I have used small areas of unusual printed or painted fabric, and have begun to introduce dip-dyed fabric into my range. (This technique involves dipping the edge of wet fabric into a dye bath and leaving it suspended; the dye is then absorbed up into the cloth, producing graded tones of the colour.)

Most of my earlier quilts were made to interchange as a bed quilt or a wallhanging; however, in recent years I have chosen to produce work only for walls. I have always enjoyed working on a large scale, and most of my quilts are around 7 feet/2 metres square. A few of my commissioned quilts have been designed in relation to specific spaces, some measuring as much as 14 by 8 feet/4.3 by 2.4 metres. Obviously, the most important aspect of a quilt is its visual impact, but these hangings can also benefit from the acoustic quality of the large echoing area in which they are displayed.

▼ **Mirrored Steps**

"Mirrored Steps" was designed from patterns that were created by setting cardboard models of steps in front of two angled mirrors. I designed a series of quilts from this imagery as part of my 3D illusion work.

The work was both pieced and quilted by machine, using both topstitching and sink stitching.

The quilt was purchased by the Shipley Art Gallery in Gateshead, Tyne and Wear, for their contemporary craft collection.

79 × 83 in/200 × 211 cm

Kate's Vase ▶

"Kate's Vase" marked the beginning of my new style of work based on paper collage studies. The looser shapes entailed a change of technique. I appliquéd all of the shapes within each block using Bondaweb (transfer fusing web) as an adhesive and cut the shapes out using templates.

I used various types of machine embroidery stitches throughout the quilt, sometimes neatly satin stitching around each shape and sometimes forming a loose network of stitching over the fabric pieces.

"Kate's Vase" is quilted with the use of a multi-needle industrial quilting machine.

This quilt was purchased by the Victoria and Albert Museum, London, and hangs in their permanent textile collection.

35 × 35 in/89 × 89 cm

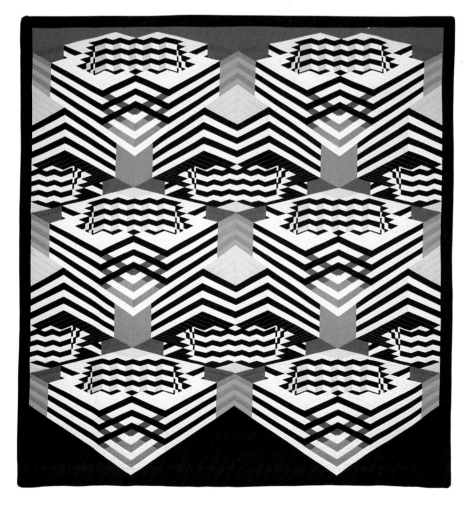

◀ Joining Forces

This quilt (detail shown overleaf) was the first large quilt of a series based on fish images. I used images of two fish, the clown sweetlips and the coral trout (shown in the paper collage, left).

  For me the quilt also symbolizes a new relationship that was beginning at this time – hence the title!

  It was purchased by the Whitworth Art Gallery, Manchester.

86 × 86 in/218 × 218 cm

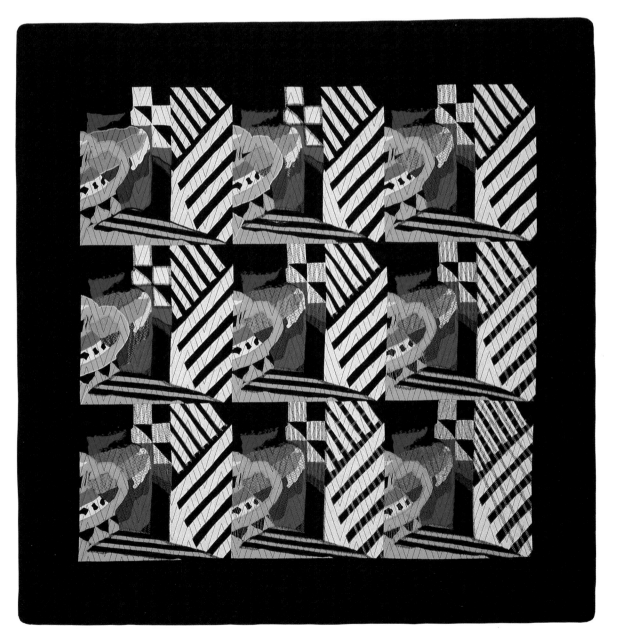

Paper and Fabric Collage

This workshop is divided into three sections: paper collage; layout design and fabric collage. The aim is to produce, first, a paper collage study from a still-life set-up, such as the one in the photograph above. This will be used as a starting point for developing a design and making a repeated-block fabric collage.

Materials

Brown paper tape or masking tape
A2 (19 × 24 in) drawing board, or piece of hardboard
A few sheets of A2 (19 × 24 in) white cartridge paper
Wallpaper paste
A selection of coloured paper
2 household paintbrushes, about 1 in/2.5 cm wide
Objects suitable for still life
A small selection of plain cotton fabrics (amounts to be determined when design is complete)
Bondaweb (transfer fusing web): 1 yard/1 metre
Lightweight (2-ounce) wadding: 1 yard/1 metre
Backing fabric: 1 yard/1 metre
Drawing and sewing materials (see page 10)

Paper Collage

1   Set up some still-life objects of your own choice, reflecting your preferences in shape, pattern and colour. These might include jars, bowls, and lengths of fabric.

2   Stretch some paper for your collage work. This is necessary to prevent the paper from buckling, so that the completed collage will dry flat.

For this, lay an A2 sheet of cartridge paper on a drawing board, wet it thoroughly with a sponge, then quickly remove excess water using the sponge wrung out. Place brown sticky paper tape around all edges, and leave the paper to dry overnight. It will dry out completely flat.

If you haven't time for this, the second best option is to use dry paper and tape firmly to the board around all edges with masking tape.

3   Mix up some wallpaper paste, using one tablespoon of powder to one jam jar full of cold water.

4   Select only a part of the still life to work from. To make this easier, cut a small square window in a sheet of paper and view through this.

5   Draw a 10 in/25 cm square on your stretched paper; make your collage within this, using coloured papers.

6   Look at the largest areas in your subject, and tear or cut these paper shapes first. To help you form the shape you require, first crease the paper where you wish to tear or cut the shape (see diagram 1). Paste the shapes down, using one brush for the wallpaper glue and one brush dry on the top surface of the paper (exactly the same technique as in applying wallpaper).

1

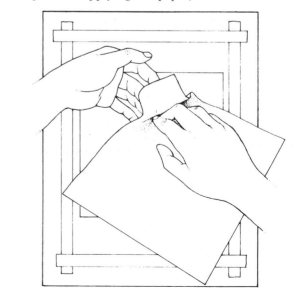

7 Gradually build up the paper collage, working towards finer detail and smaller pieces at the end (see diagram 2).

2

Layout Design

1 Draw a 5 in/13 cm square on a sheet of tracing paper, move this over the paper collage and select the area you find most pleasing (see diagram 3).

3

2 Trace the shapes within the square onto the tracing paper.

3 Turn the tracing over, and draw over the lines with a soft pencil.

4 Trace 9 of these blocks, right way up, onto plain paper, and another 4 or 5 in reverse or mirror image (see diagram 4). (After every few times, you will need to go over the lines again with the soft pencil.)

4

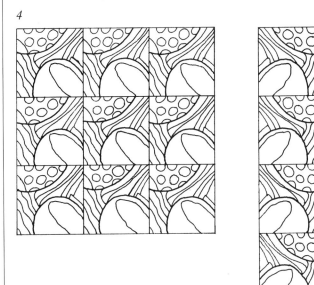

5 Cut out all these blocks and rearrange them into a good repeat pattern, using only 9 blocks for the finished design. There are many possibilities. Diagram 5 shows some standard ways of repeating square blocks.

5

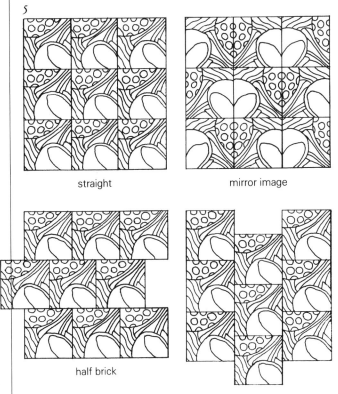

straight   mirror image

half brick

half drop

6 When you have achieved the best result, paste it down onto a sheet of paper or cardboard. This is your layout design pattern to follow.

A few thoughts when doing this exercise:

1 What makes a good repeat block design?

- One that flows from block to block, thereby losing the original square image.
- One that creates an overall pattern with different size and density of shapes.
- Two equal sections could be used successfully, particularly using positive and negative shapes, as shown in diagram 6.
- A lopsided image will repeat much more interestingly than a block with a central image.

6

rotating blocks

2 It can be helpful to colour one layout design sheet in black and white only, as an alternative to using all the colours from your paper collage study. Limiting your options to a choice of only black and white can be a useful tool to encourage clear design thoughts. Try this as an alternative project.

Fabric Collage

This part of the workshop consists of making the original design block in fabric and assembling 9 of these blocks to make the complete fabric collage.

1 Look at the amount of detail in your 5 in/13 cm block design, and decide whether it can be made up in fabric on this scale. You may need to enlarge the block. For example, you might wish to make it twice as large: 10 in/26 cm square.

To scale up a design, first draw a regular square grid over the block and draw another grid twice as large i.e. each square is twice the size of the original. Transfer the image from square 1:A on the 5 in/13 cm block to square 1:A on the larger drawing, and systematically work through all the squares until you have the whole image drawn. This will give you the same proportions as your original (see diagram 7). The amount you enlarge the second grid will determine the overall enlargement.

7

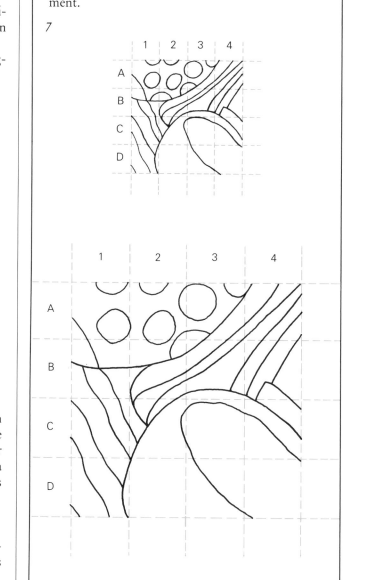

2 Make a tracing of the full-size block and the shapes within it. Add a line ½ in/1.2 cm outside all edges for seam allowance.

3 Refer to your paper collage for the colours. Observe which is the largest area of colour on the block; use this colour for your base block. For example, if black predominates, cut the base block from black fabric. Number all the shapes except those which are black on the tracing (see diagram 8). All these shapes will be applied to the background fabric.

In this simple fabric collage all the shapes meet edge to edge. It is possible, of course, to cut shapes that overlap (drawing templates accordingly). However, note that the Bondaweb (transfer fusing web) makes the fabric thicker, and so it is best to avoid using too many layers of fabric.

8

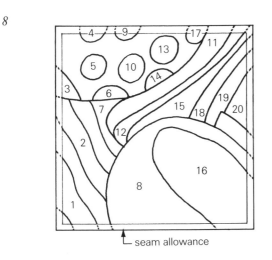

⌊ seam allowance

4 Cut one base block the size of the square, including the seam allowance.

5 To make the templates, trace each separate shape from the tracing onto thin cardboard. The ½ in/1.2 cm seam allowance must be included in those templates that are placed on the edges of the block – for example, Template 8 (see diagram 9).

9

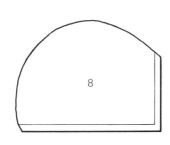

6 Number the templates to correspond to the numbers on the tracing.

7 Choose the fabric for each shape, and cut out a small square (approximately 8–10 in/20–25 cm) or rectangle of each colour to be used.

8 Cut pieces of Bondaweb (transfer fusing web) about ¼ in/6 mm smaller than the fabric shapes. Iron this onto the chosen fabric with a hot, dry iron, making sure you iron it on the smooth, paper side.

9 Place each template, reverse side up (check this against the design), on the Bondaweb side of the fabric and draw around it. Cut these out.

10 Peel the backing paper from the cut-out shapes and position the fabric pieces on the base cloth (see diagram 10). Use the traced design to check the correct position of the pieces, then iron the shapes onto the base block. This completes one block.

10

11 Make up 8 more identical/mirror image blocks in the same way, following your repeating design.

12 To finish the collage, you can use decorative machine embroidery over the shapes on each separate block, then piece the blocks together and quilt. Alternatively, you can piece the blocks together first and incorporate the machine embroidery as part of the machine quilting.

In either case it would be necessary to quilt by machine rather than by hand, because the Bondaweb (transfer fusing web) makes the fabric a little too stiff for hand quilting.

Assemble the three layers – the top appliquéd fabric, the wadding and the backing fabric – to create a sandwich. Cut wadding and backing fabric a little larger than the top cloth and trim to shape after the stitching is complete. Tack and stitch through all layers.

Depending on the size of the work, it could be used for a cushion cover, for example, or a wallhanging.

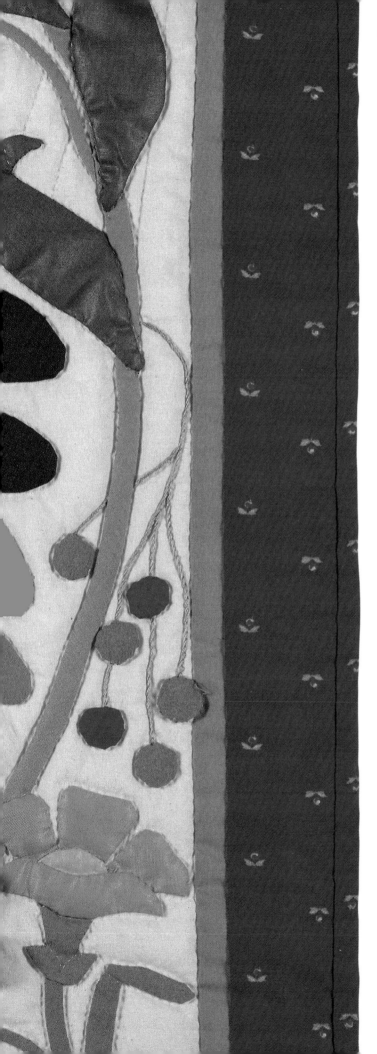

Appliqué

Jenny Dove

Jenny Dove's introduction to quiltmaking was through appliqué, which, including the technique of reverse appliqué, has remained her favourite medium through ten years of quiltmaking and teaching. Since 1986 she has taught sampler quiltmaking at Walford Mill Craft Centre in Wimborne, Dorset, and has held workshops at her home in the Dorset countryside.

Sources and Approaches

Colour is the dominant ingredient in planning my designs, and I am happiest working with pure cotton, generally in solid colours. Like most quiltmakers, I have built up a large store of fabrics over the years, and I enjoy the discipline of using what I have, rather than buying fabrics especially for a project. I organize my fabrics colour-wise on open shelves for convenience when searching for a particular pattern or colour. Between five and ten different colours go into a typical quilt.

Shopping for fabrics is a special pleasure on holidays in France, where market stalls often yield colours and patterns different from those seen in England. Recently I realized that my work was marked by a predominance of greens and corals, so I decided to break away into Provençal blues and yellows in my last quilt, "Sunshine Sampler", combining French fabrics with a design inspired by a trip to Portugal. Such stimuli help to keep one's work fresh.

Closer to home, the designs found in English Jacobean crewel embroidery are another source of inspiration. I love their fantastic shapes and curling tendrils, the exotic flowers growing from hillocks, the bizarre birds and insects. For these complex designs, I tack the shapes to the background without tacking the edges under first in the usual way, and I then turn under the edge with the needle as I go. This method is used in Hawaiian and Baltimore quilt appliqué.

To illustrate new techniques or designs for my students, I have made many small items, such as a variety of cushions (strip-pieced, quilted, appliquéd and reverse appliquéd); bags of different sizes – from large Seminole strip totes to small evening bags in silk using herringbone tucks and trimmed with tiny pearls.

I love the effect of quilting on clothing and have made many waist-coats, jackets and coats. Some of these are of silk, which beautifully enhances the texture of the quilting; others are in cotton or fine wool. I have adapted a paper pattern for a Turkish-style coat, adding random machine quilting on the body which complements the fine hand quilt-ing on the borders.

On a visit to California some years ago I attended classes on making molas by Charlotte Patera – an authority on this subject. Molas are in-tricately worked panels of reverse appliqué often made into blouses, by the Kuna Indians of the San Blas Islands, off the coast of Panama. It is a complex and time-consuming technique, but fascinating, and one I have continued to explore in a simpler form. Essentially, reverse appliqué consists of placing two or more layers of fabric together and then cutting away upper fabric layers in the chosen design to reveal those underneath. The effect can be quite dramatic and, if made in vivid colours, evocative of stained glass. The technique lends itself to endless possibilities, whether used on its own or combined with simple appliqué. I sometimes use, as the bottom layers, strips of different col-ours to create a delicate or rainbow-like effect. One of my favourite motifs for reverse appliqué is the dove, which I have used in small hangings and as a quilt block.

Gardens of Delight
(previous page)

This wallhanging was commissioned by the Walford Mill Craft Centre to serve as the poster for an exhibition of quilts entitled "Gardens of Delight". After much trial and error, helpful suggestions from my husband, and hours of happy experimenting with fabric textures – chintzes, silks, crêpes and sequins – I created this garden, whose "Delights" include an exotic bird on a Tree of Life, grapes, strawberries, butterflies and flamboyant flowers, under an ever-shining sun.

24 × 32 in/60 × 181 cm

Sunshine Sampler ▶

I prepared this quilt as a teaching aid, including as many patchwork, appliqué and quilting techniques as possible. Among them are hexagons, tumbling blocks, Hawaiian and reverse appliqué, Log Cabin, Clamshells, Seminole patchwork, Amish quilting, Roman Stripe and curved-seam piecing. The motifs include a dove, a house, and a Celtic motif adapted from a palace window in Sintra, Portugal. Completing the twenty blocks, then joining them with blue borders, quilted with a cable design, took only ten weeks – my shortest time ever for a quilt. Its name was inspired by the many happy summer sunshine-filled hours I spent in the garden working on it.

82 × 82 in/209 × 209 cm

New Zealand Memories

Each block of this sampler quilt represents a memory of the year, 1985, that my husband and I spent in New Zealand – he teaching secondary school; I, quiltmaking. It was constructed by the quilt-as-you-go, or lap-quilting method. Among the stylized images to be found in it are a thistle and a schematic representation of an eightsome reel, evocative of the Scottish dancing group we belonged to; giant Kauri trees, ferns and manuka (the last worked in clamshell patchwork), suggesting the New Zealand bush; a design from a Maori headband; palm trees; baskets of oranges, worked in Seminole patchwork; and kiwi birds (included somewhat wishfully, as we never managed to see any). The old mill wheel in the centre represents the craft school in England where I used the quilt for teaching.

I was delighted when this quilt won an award at the National (U.K.) Patchwork Championships in 1988.

66 × 93 in/167 × 236 cm

Tudor Rose Cushion ▶

The Tudor rose has become one of my favourite motifs for reverse appliqué. It has a narrow area surrounding each petal, just sufficient for the turnings on each side to be sewn into place. The design was drawn onto the top blue fabric and a single gold layer was placed beneath, with a circle of deeper yellow exactly in the centre. The green leaves were eased into position at the end. I quilted around the reversed layer, giving an extra dimension to the top layer, and also closely in the centre. The tiny yellow strip was folded into the border for additional linear and textural interest.

16 × 16 in/40.5 × 40.5 cm

◀ Mulberry Bush

The preliminary work on this wallhanging proved the ideal handwork to take on a cycling and camping trip to Normandy, when space was at a premium. While relaxing on the beach, I tacked under the edges of the sixty leaves and gathered the edges of thirty small chintz circles to make the berries. On returning home, I prepared the background of natural calico, applied the tree trunk, leaves, berries and bird, and finally quilted around each appliquéd piece.

28 × 28 in/72 × 72 cm

Summer Flowers Crewel Design Cushion

A book of crewel embroidery designs that I found has proved a rich source of inspiration for appliqué. Although many of the shapes are too difficult to be adapted for this purpose, I have managed to create seven usable designs. Among the more detailed of these is "Summer Flowers". I like the way that the turn of a petal reveals a deeper shade on the underside, and that the basically simple yellow flowers gain a solidity when the detail lines on them are quilted. I have used this block, which measures 12 in/30.5 cm square, for a cushion cover, measuring 16 in/40 cm square.

Materials

For the background, piece of good-quality calico, 12½ in/32 cm square

For the appliqué, scraps of medium-weight, closely woven cotton in shades of blue and yellow or other chosen colours (may include small prints)

For the border and backing, cotton fabric, any width, in yellow or chosen colour: ¾ yard/60 cm

Stranded cotton floss in colours to blend with fabrics

Template plastic

Lightweight (2-ounce) polyester wadding: ½ yard/50 cm

Cushion pad, 18 in/45 cm square

Drawing and sewing materials (see page 10)

Preparing the Design

1 Enlarge the design given in diagram 1, following the method described on page 42, so that it measures 12 in/30.5 cm square. Go over the lines of the enlarged drawing with a dark pen. This is the master copy.

1

2 Centre the design under the background fabric, and secure both with sticky tape to a flat surface (a sunny window is ideal for this, especially for a dense-coloured fabric, when you will need to have a light source shining from behind the pattern). Trace the design onto the background fabric, using a sharp but soft pencil to avoid dragging. Omit detailed lines on the leaves and petals. The shapes serve as guides for positioning the pieces.

3 On the master copy, number all the shapes requiring templates, ignoring stems and tendrils. Place a piece of template plastic over each numbered shape, trace carefully with a sharp pencil and mark the number (see diagram 2).

2

4 Cut out the templates (use curved nail scissors where they may help to cut smooth curves). Keep the templates together in a container until needed.

Working the Appliqué
1 Prepare the fabrics to be used (see page 11). Place each template right side up on the right side of the chosen fabric; the numbers will make it clear which side of the template is the right side; if turned over they would produce a mirror image shape. Position the template so that the fabric grain runs vertically and horizontally, so that the grain will match that of the background as closely as possible. Draw around the template carefully with a sharp pencil or coloured marking pencil (see diagram 3). At this point you may wish to sketch in any

3

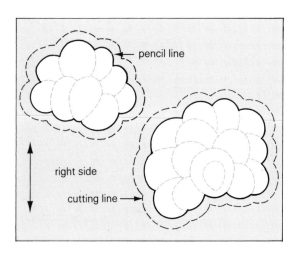

details to be embroidered or quilted on the shapes. The pencil lines will be covered by the stitching.

2 Cut out each shape, leaving a scant ¼ in/5 mm around the drawn line. Pin it in position on the background, checking with the master copy and making sure that the drawn line on the shape matches that on the background. Any pieces that will be overlapped must be positioned before those that overlap them, for example piece 11 should be pinned in place before piece 10.

3 When all the shapes have been positioned, tack them lightly to the background, no closer than ¼ in/5 mm in from the drawn line to allow the edge to be turned under; work on a flat surface.

4 Cut the stems for the design on the true bias (i.e. the strips should be cut at 45° to the grain line), making the main stems ¾ in/2 cm wide and the others ½ in/1.2 cm wide. Fold over one long edge, then fold the other over it (see diagram 4), and tack the edges in place without pinning first.
  Do not press the prepared strip; it will then bend in whatever position you wish. Pin and tack the stems to the background, placing them so that the raw edge is on the underneath. Check that one end lies well under the edge of the flower or leaf; the other end should either flow into the border or be neatly turned under, depending on the design. Small stems and tendrils may be embroidered later.

4

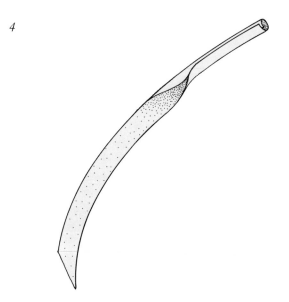

5 For small circles, make a cardboard template (a thimble may be useful for this) and use it to mark the fabric. Cut out the circles, adding ¼ in/5 mm margins. Work small gathering stitches close to the edge (see diagram 5a). Re-insert the cardboard circle, and draw up the threads (diagram 5b). Press carefully (a plastic template could melt at this stage!). When the fabric is cool, remove the circle. The result is a perfect circle, ready to be applied to the background.

5a

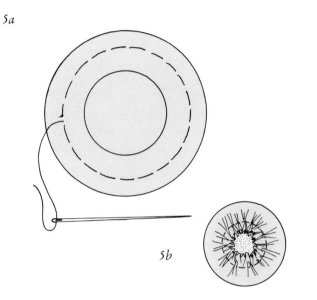

5b

6 Before sewing the shapes down, snip into their seam allowance along all concave curved edges – *not* the convex curves – cutting right up to the drawn line but not into it. The more exaggerated the curve, the more snips are necessary (see diagram 6). Snip also into any inward angles. The snipping makes it possible to turn the edges under.

6

7 Using a single strand of sewing thread to match the fabric shape, sew each shape to the background as shown, sweeping the needle towards you to tuck the edge underneath, just concealing the drawn line. Hold the shape in position with the thumb, and stitch so that the thread goes from the fold of the fabric straight down into the background, then comes up into the fold of the

fabric, about ¼ in/5 mm farther on (see diagram 7). Keep the stitches very firm, without dragging, so that the shape does not "float" on the surface. Tuck under only a little fabric at a time, in order to keep a smooth curve. For sharp points, first fold down the tip, fold one side over it and then the other, and hold in position with the thumb until it is stitched. Any raw edges that will be covered are left raw to keep the surface smooth.

7

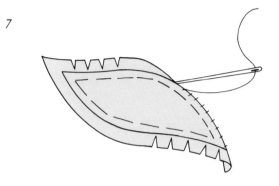

8 When all the shapes and stems have been applied, embroider the tendrils in stem stitch (see diagram 8), using 2 or 3 strands of embroidery thread and keeping the curves as smooth as possible. You can add as much or as little embroidery as you wish. The details on the flowers can be embroidered at this point or quilted later.

8

Making Up the Cover
9 For the border, cut 4 strips, each 2½ × 16½ in/6.2 × 41.2 cm. Sew them to the edges of the appliqué, taking ¼ in/6 mm seam allowance. Either mitre the corners or leave them straight. Press the work lightly on the wrong side. Layer with wadding and backing fabric, pin and tack firmly. Quilt around all pieces and any detail lines on flowers or leaves. Piping can be added to the edges at this point. Cut a piece of the yellow fabric 16½ in/ 41.2 cm square. Place the bordered appliqué and the yellow fabric right sides together, and stitch, leaving part of the seam free. Turn through to the right side and fit in the cushion pad. Slipstitch the remaining sides together. Alternatively, a zip can be inserted into the back for ease of removal of the cushion pad.

Mariner's Compass

Margaret Hughes

Since childhood, Margaret Hughes has enjoyed sewing and collecting fabrics, but it was only after the last of her four children started school that she discovered the pleasures of patchwork. What began as merely a pastime to fill some spare hours has now become "an addiction", but one that has brought her great satisfaction and "a wealth of marvellous friends".

Sources and Approaches

In my work I have experimented with a wide spectrum of traditional patterns, which best suit my home and lifestyle. I sometimes piece by machine, sometimes by hand. As a busy housewife I appreciate the speed of the American block method, but I also enjoy doing traditional English patchwork from time to time. The familiar hexagon has design possibilities that we have not yet explored to the full.

Appliqué is a technique I sometimes use for pictures and wall-hangings; these, too, are quilted. All my work, whether pieced or appliquéd, is quilted by hand.

Fabrics are a main source of ideas, and often serve as the stimulus for a new piece of work. I prefer to work with fabrics which are made of natural fibres.

Another source of inspiration is the work of other quilters. There are many gifted professionals in our craft today, who are setting very high standards of design.

I enjoy teaching Mariner's Compass, using the method described here, which is relatively simple and yields excellent results even with beginners. I made my first Mariner's Compass in 1983, as part of a wallhanging, which I still own. Although the compass has limited use – being a single motif rather than a repeatable block – it does have considerable appeal, especially for people who are fascinated by ships and the sea. The 32-point compass shown here can be adapted in various ways to resemble some of the original designs found on old maps.

My Friendly Mariner
(previous page)

This was my first attempt at drawing and sewing a mariner's compass. Drawn with the aid of a pencil and a piece of string, it is full of inaccuracies but I'm still fond of it and it inspired me to try again. It is made entirely with Liberty lawn fabrics.

39 × 41 in/99 × 104 cm

▼ **Blue Cushion by Kate George; Autumn Coloured Cushion by Jean Mellows**

Two cushions made by students at mariner's compass workshops, each carefully drawn and beautifully sewn.

each 16 × 16 in/40.5 × 40.5 cm

△ Sail Away

The main design of the quilt is made from a 6 in/15 cm block called Sail Boat. This close-up shows the border where the compass has been cut into quarters at each corner.

23 × 25 in/58 × 63.5 cm

△ A Cushion Quilt

The cushion cover acts as a bag which secretly houses a small lap quilt. It is made with cotton fabrics.

15 × 15 in/38 × 38 cm

Two Handkerchief Cases ▶

The pink and blue case made from silks has appliquéd flowers in the centre. The black, pink and lemon case has a Victorian feel, it is made from a mixture of cotton, silk and crêpe de chine fabrics.

each 9½ in/24 cm in diameter

Round Cushion

The Amish American Quilts inspired me to use these colours. I added a multicoloured piping to give extra interest to the finished edges.

13 in/33 cm in diameter

Constructing a Mariner's Compass

The following instructions are for drafting and sewing a Mariner's Compass approximately 13 in/33 cm in diameter. This can then be used in a cushion cover, wallhanging or other project.

Materials
Fabrics in 5 colours: ¼ yard/20 cm of each

Cork, polystyrene or pin board, approximately 12 in/30 cm square (a size to fit on your lap is ideal)

Drawing and sewing equipment (see page 10), including a compass and 3 coloured pencils: blue, green and red

Drafting the Compass
There are various ways to draw a compass. I favour the folding method, which is simple and does not involve any complicated mathematics. It is good to be able to draw your own compass, rather than relying on those given in books, since this enables you to make whatever size you like to suit the project you have in mind.

1 Using the compass, set to a radius of 6½ in/16.5 cm, draw a circle 13 in/33 cm in diameter on a sheet of thin drawing paper; we will call this the outer circle. If your compass is not large enough, use a plate or other round object of this diameter. Cut out the circle.

2 If you have not used a compass, find the centre of the circle by folding it into four quarters. Now draw a small circle in the centre – to be called the inner circle – 3¼ in/8 cm in diameter. When deciding the size of the inner circle the rule to remember is: the smaller the circle, the thinner the points; the larger the circle, the fatter the points.

3 Fold the circle twice more, making 8 equal divisions.

4 Open the circle and lay it on a flat surface. Using the blue pencil, mark two dots on each fold line, one on the outer circle, one on the inner circle.

5 Using the ruler, join one of the dots on the outer circle to the next dot to the right on the inner circle, and draw a blue line connecting the two dots (see diagram 1). Continuing around the circle clockwise, join all the remaining outer and inner dots as shown.

1

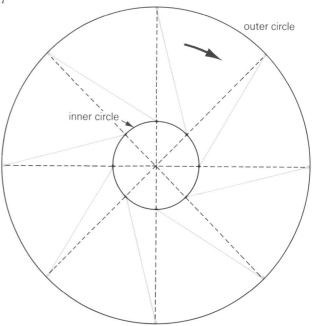

outer circle

inner circle

6 Repeat Step 5 anticlockwise (see diagram 2). You have now completed the first 8 points of the compass.

2

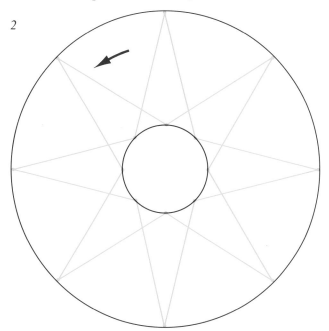

7 Now fold the circle 8 more times, to make 16 divisions. Open out the circle, and make dots as before but on new fold lines, using the green pencil. Using the ruler and the green pencil, join a green outer dot to the adjacent green inner dot, but stopping when you reach the first blue line. Continue around the circle, first clockwise, then anticlockwise (see diagram 3). The compass now has 16 points.

The remaining 16 points are marked without folding, since this number of folds would be difficult to handle.

3

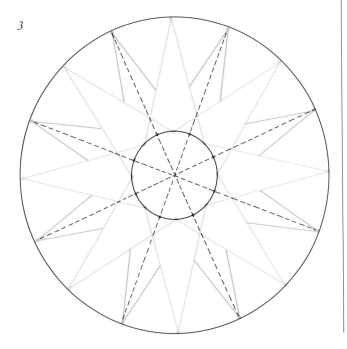

8 Place the ruler over the centre of the circle, so that its edge goes precisely through two points where blue and green points meet (see diagram 4). Using the red pencil, mark 4 dots, 2 on the outer circle and 2 on the inner. Continue in this way all around the compass until you have marked 16 dots equally spaced around both circles.

4

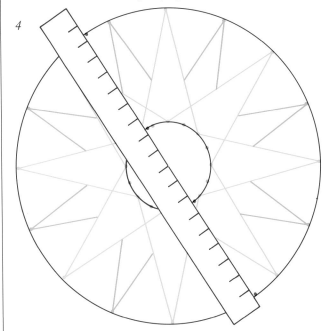

9 Using the ruler, join a red outside dot to a red dot on the inner circle, 2 dots away from the one directly opposite. If you were to use the adjacent dots, the new points would be too narrow. With red pencil, draw each point around the circle, stopping at the blue and green lines (see diagram 5). The compass design is now complete.

5

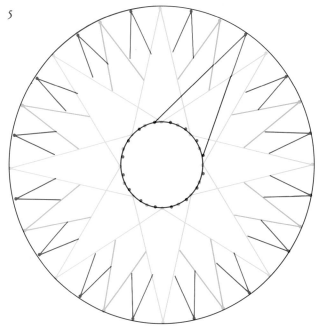

My Favourite Basket

*Made from cotton fabrics
throughout, this workbasket is
lined inside with added pockets
and topped with a mariner's
compass lid.*

15½ in/39.5 cm in diameter

Making the Patchwork

Books often instruct you to use a set of templates, one
for each shape in the compass, but I have found that this
generally causes problems when fitting the fabric shapes
together. I have therefore developed my own method,
which many of my students have also used successfully.
I use the drawn paper compass as my pattern, cutting
and using *every* segment as a separate template. The
reason for this is that the paper segments will vary, if
only by a tiny amount; by cutting each fabric segment to
match a particular paper segment you eliminate fitting
problems. The paper compass is dismantled, while at the
same time the fabric compass is assembled. Follow these
steps and you will find you develop a rhythm of cutting
segments, pinning them on a board, then removing and
stitching.

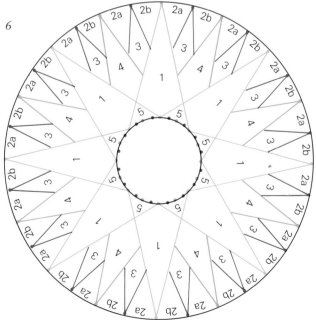

1   Number every segment 1 to 5, as shown in diagram
6, noting that number 2 is subdivided into 2a and 2b.

2 Chose your five fabrics and decide where you are going to use them in the design.

3 Make a reference chart, listing the numbers 1, 2a, 2b, 3, 4, and 5, and attach a snippet of the chosen fabric for each of these shapes alongside each number. Note that 2a and 2b use the same fabric (see diagram 7). Assemble all your fabrics (prepared as described on page 11) and other tools and materials, so that they are within easy reach.

4 Cut out your first template: any number 1 segment on the circle. Using this as your template, place it, numbered side down on the wrong side of the appropriate fabric, and mark around it. Cut out the fabric shape, adding the usual ¼ in/6 mm seam allowance on all edges. Discard the paper segment 1.

5 Pin the fabric segment 1 to the polystyrene or cork board.

6 Moving clockwise around the circle, cut paper segment 2a. Mark and cut this from the chosen fabric and pin it to the board. Discard the paper template. *Continue to discard each paper template once it has been used.*

7 Cut paper segment 3, and mark and cut it from fabric. Pin it to the board.

8 Remove segments 3 and 2a from the board and stitch, with right sides together and making sure that you join the correct edges. Use a fine running stitch with an occasional backstitch. Finger press the seam toward the darker fabric.

9 Cut paper segment 2b from the chosen fabric. Sew segment 2b to segments 3 and 2a, as before. Pin this section to the board.

10 Cut paper segment 4 from the chosen fabric. Sew segment 4 to segments 2a-3-2b along the edge; finger press.

11 Join this whole section to the fabric segment 1, along edges 2a, 3 and 4; finger press. Pin this section to the board.

12 Now cut out the following segments, 2a, 3 and 2b; mark, cut out and join as before. Sew this section to the first one; finger press the seam. Pin this whole section to the board.

13 Cut out segment 5 from the chosen fabric; pin it to the board.

14 Cut out the next segment 1 from the chosen fabric. Sew segment 5 to segment 1, making sure to join the correct edge of segment 5, because the curved edge must later be joined to the inner circle.

15 Now sew this section (5 and 1) to the previously joined section in one straight line. You have now completed the section shown in colour in diagram 7.

7

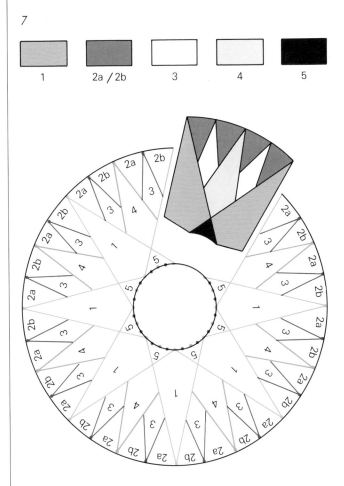

16 Continue in a clockwise direction, cutting and sewing the segments together until you reach the last segment 5. Sew this to the base of the first segment 1. Join the resulting straight edge to the adjacent straight edge. Press the work. Press all the seams in one direction unless this would mean that a dark seam would show through onto a light fabric.

17 Finally, cut the inner circle from a fabric of your choice. This piece can either be inserted into the centre and sewn with right sides facing, to the other edges, or appliquéd over the edges, using a fine slip stitch. Give a final press to the work.

Now your compass is completed and ready to be incorporated into your chosen project.

Whirlies

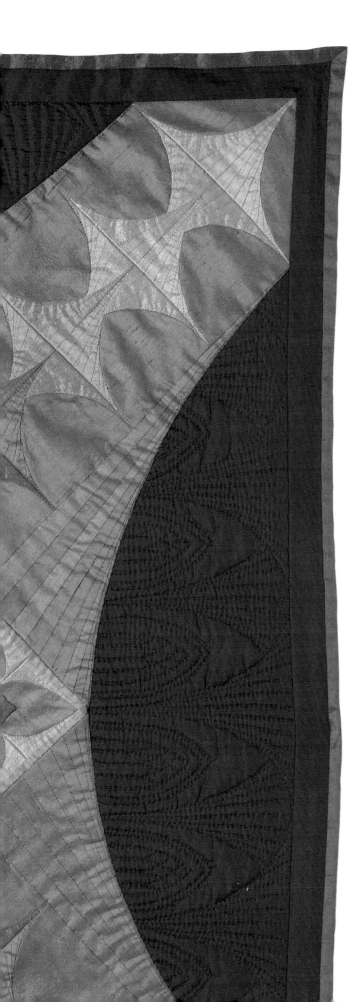

Rita Humphry

Patchwork is Rita Humphry's third career. She started off as a musician – mainly as a keyboard artist – which she credits with having given her stamina, good powers of concentration and a passion for accuracy. She then married and raised a family, which added ''patience, more stamina, organization and how to improvise''. In about 1980 she started doing patchwork as an occasional refuge from the demands of running a large household. This led to her attending a teaching course. Since then she has worked as a freelance quiltmaker and teacher.

Sources and Approaches

Although I very occasionally make wholecloth quilts by hand, I normally work in a machine-pieced variation of the Log Cabin technique that produces illusions of curves. This technique is an invention of my own, arrived at during my time at Loughborough, and I have been exploring its possibilities ever since. The variation of pattern seems almost endless; I am continually fascinated by the way completely straight lines can be placed in such ways as to create sinuous arabesques or apparently perfect circles. It is a time-consuming method and requires extreme accuracy in both drafting and construction, but I find that it satisfies the strong need I have for order and complexity.

A paradoxical aspect of the way I work is that I do not actually like using a sewing machine very much. This is one reason why my designs often include unpieced areas, which demand to be filled with elaborate quilting or embroidery. Whenever possible I do this by hand, but sometimes a machine technique is a better solution. I also use the machine to modify colours or to create texture.

Some of my work is purely geometric and the result of asking, "What would happen if …?" Other pieces have been inspired by ecclesiastical architecture. I love churches and cathedrals and often cause consternation by lying flat on my back to study the vaulting. Churches are simply crammed with beautiful shapes, colours and textures. Just think of the carvings in stone and wood; the shapes of the windows and the colours of the glass and the patterns they make on

Hereford

(previous page)

This is the only piece I have made that started with a piece of fabric. I happened to pass by the cathedral as the sun came out after a heavy spring shower. The colour of the stone was exactly that of a piece of pink silk I had been hoarding for years. The design was inspired by vaulting in the cathedral. The patchwork has machine-corded quilting and is embroidered. The burgundy background is hand-quilted.

38½ × 38½ in/98 × 98 cm

Mirage ▶

I liked the idea of a series of related grids piled up on top of each other, but I had great difficulty arriving at a suitable colour scheme. Eventually I put the warmer colours on the bottom layers and the coldest on the top layer, hoping to create a shimmer effect. The black background (see below) has close lines of machine stitching in an ombré thread of cream, rust and dark brown.

30 × 38 in/76 × 97 cm

◀ Corona

I hit a recurrent problem with this quilt. I like black as a background colour, but find that plain black is too hard and stark. Every time I try, I end up having to do acres of machine embroidery to soften it. This time I used a twin needle with black thread in one of the bobbins and purple in the other and did a very simple V-shaped pattern.

32 × 32 in/181 × 181 cm

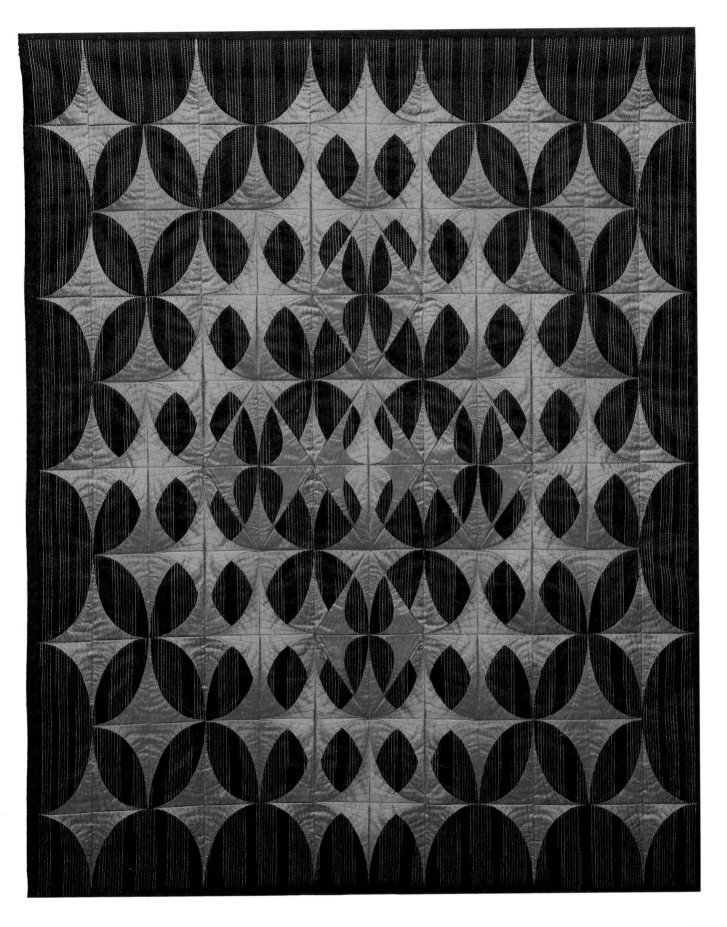

the floors – not to mention the patterns of the tiles and stones them-selves. One could make dozens of quilts out of a single cathedral – if only a week had ten days!

Another source of inspiration is the strongly geometric structure apparent in some natural forms. And then there is the colour – the rose-hued stone of Hereford Cathedral; acres of heather on an Irish mountain lit by the evening sun; the variegation of a box turtle and the iridescent skin of a torpid snake, which can change from a dull greeny-brown to the brilliance of emeralds, sapphires and lapis lazuli.

I always work in silk. Not only do I love the feel of it and the bril-liance of the colours, but the nature of the technique I use makes it the obvious fabric. Each curve is achieved by setting straight strips of fab-ric, cut on the straight grain, at a slightly different angle from the pre-vious strip. This difference affects the way the light is reflected from each strip and creates a diversity of tone and a feeling of movement that would be far less dramatic if cotton were used. Because of the complexity of the patterns, I tend to use mainly solid colours, with some shot and striped fabrics – usually dupion or taffeta. For the quilted and embroidered areas I use organzas, tulle, Habutai silk, dyed fleece and a wide variety of silk and metallic threads.

Most of my work is fairly small-scale and purely decorative. Some, like the cathedral quilts, which are intended to be hung on walls, are on average 3–4 feet/90 cm–1.2 metres square. The largest I have made is 51 in/130 cm square. Other pieces, like the snakes and the tortoise, measure only about 8 × 12 in/20 × 30 cm and are mounted, glazed and framed. Every so often, I satisfy my preference for handwork by mak-ing a double bed-sized wholecloth quilt. For me there is no pleasure quite so addictive as hand quilting.

▲ **Tortoiseshell**
(detail)

The four blocks with the shield shapes were made by layering organza over hand-dyed fleece and were an attempt to reproduce the mottled effect of worked tortoiseshell. Each "spiral" block measures 2⅜ in/6 cm at the widest point and contains 73 tiny pieces of fabric.

8¼ × 11½ in/21 × 29 cm

Comeragh
(previous pages)

This quilt was inspired by the pink and purple heather among grey rocks in the Comeragh Mountains, Ireland. Some of the central diamonds are hand-dyed Habutai with corded quilting, others are machine-embroidered in metallic thread on combed "fleece". The grey-striped fabric has extra rows of machine stitching for the border.

36 × 50½ in/91 × 128 cm

A Whirly Block

Whirlies are a form of Log Cabin made on a foundation; it is ideally a machine technique but quite possible to do by hand. My first Whirly quilt, "Spiral Strip", featured a border pattern, based on a 4 in/10 cm square, that looked like folded ribbon.

The instructions that follow are for making a single block of that border. The effectiveness of the design emerges fully only when several blocks are joined together.

To make the block you will need a neutral-coloured fabric for the background and 4 graded tones of a colour for the "ribbon". Use unpatterned silk or lightweight cotton. The fabric should be able to take a good crease. The quantities given are for a single block. To estimate the amount of fabric needed for a number of blocks, multiply the number by the quantities given under "Cutting the Strips".

Materials

Plain-coloured fabrics, any width, in 4 tones of the same colour: ⅛ yard/10 cm of each
Neutral-coloured fabric, any width: ⅛ yard/10 cm
Piece of Stitch 'n' Tear or lightweight sew-in interfacing (optional), approximately 5 in/12 cm square
Drawing and sewing materials (see page 10, including a compass)

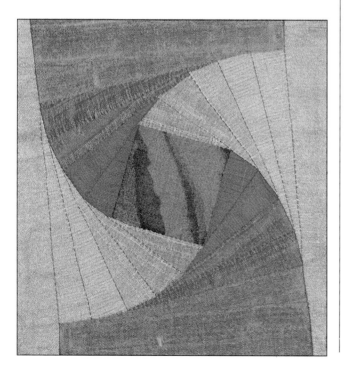

Drafting the Pattern

1 Draw a 4 in/10 cm square on a piece of tracing paper. Label the corner points A1, A2, A3 and A4, starting at the top left-hand corner and working around in a clockwise direction.

2 Set the compass to ½ in/1.2 cm. Place the point of the compass at the corner labelled A1 and make a mark along the line A1–A2. Continue around the square clockwise, setting the compass point on each corner and making a mark on lines A2–A3, A3–A4 and A4–A1 in turn (see diagram 1). The marking can also be done with a ruler, by measuring and making a dot ½ in/1.2 cm from each corner – but take care. If using a compass, make sure the measurement remains ½ in/1.2 cm; if it is greater, the curve will extend too far down.

1
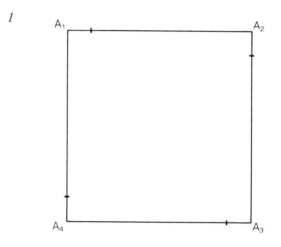

3 Label the points just marked B1, B2, B3 and B4. Join up the B points, forming a new "B" square which is tilted within the original "A" square (see diagram 2).

2
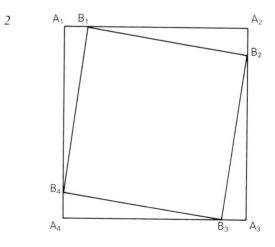

4 Set the compass point on B1, and make a mark along the line B1–B2. Continue around the B square in a clockwise direction, making marks on each line as before.

Label the new points C1, C2, C3 and C4. Join them up to form a C square (diagram 3). Continue in this way until you have made 6 new squares in all, the smallest measuring 1¼ in/3.2 cm. (You need not label all the corners once you have established the procedure.)

3

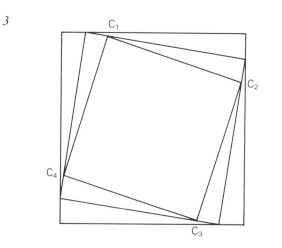

5 Add a ½ in/1.2 cm seam allowance all around the original square (see diagram 4). This completes the pattern for the Whirly block. The finished block will be a mirror image of this tracing.

4

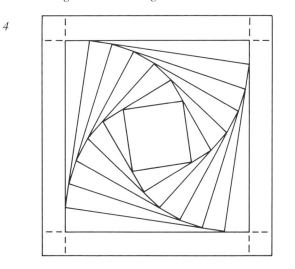

Making the Foundation Piece

The pattern must now be transferred to the foundation square. The simplest way is to make a photocopy of the pattern and sew the strips directly onto the paper; this is later torn away. Alternatively, you can trace the pattern onto Stitch 'n' Tear (if you are machine sewing) or lightweight sew-in non-woven interfacing (for hand sewing), as follows:

1 Place the pattern on a firm, flat surface, and, using masking tape, fix Stitch 'n' Tear or interfacing over it.

2 Using a ruler and different-coloured pens to indicate the outside edge, seamlines and stitching lines, carefully trace the pattern. Fine felt-tip pens or ballpoint pens are more suitable markers than pencils, which will not show up once you start sewing.

3 Finally, add any information you might need about colours and order of sewing strips (see diagram 5).

5

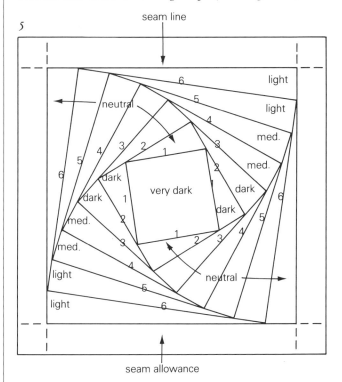

Cutting the Strips

Cut 4 strips and one square on the straight grain, to the following measurements:

Colour 1a (very dark)	2 in/5 cm square
Colour 1b (dark)	1¼ × 8 in/3.2 × 20 cm strip
Colour 1c (medium)	1¼ × 12 in/3.2 × 30 cm strip
Colour 1d (light)	1¼ × 16 in/3.2 × 40 cm strip
Colour 2 (neutral)	1¼ × 36 in/3.2 × 90 cm strip

Sewing the Block

All the sewing of a Whirly block is done on the lines marked on the foundation piece, which is the wrong side. The strips are placed on the unmarked right side.

1 With the foundation piece marked side up, insert a pin at each corner of the centre shape. They should extend about ½ in/1 cm on the other side.

2 Turn the foundation piece over, trying not to dislodge the pins. Hook the 2 in/5 cm square of Colour 1a, right side up, over the points of the pins so that the seam allowance is fairly evenly distributed (see diagram 6).

6

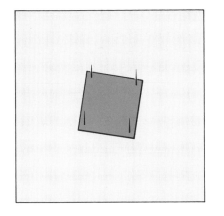

3 Push the pins right through, and push the centre square down so that it is lying flat against the foundation. Tack it in place and remove the pins.

4 Start with the shortest strip, Colour 1b (dark). Insert pins at either end of the seamline (see diagram 7), turn over foundation piece, and hook one end of the strip, right side *down*, over the upper pin so that there is at least ¼ in/6 mm seam allowance to the right of the pin and also above it. Smooth the strip along and hook it over the lower pin so that there is ¼ in/6 mm seam allowance to the right (see diagram 8). Trim off the rest of the long strip, leaving ¼ in/6 mm seam allowance below the lower pin. Secure it in place with a pin. (Don't worry if the raw edges are not exactly aligned.)

7

8

5 Turn the foundation piece wrong side up, and stitch along the marked seamline, stopping and starting a stitch or two beyond the actual marked line. Diagram 9 shows the completed seam from the right side. Trim any surplus 1a fabric level with the strip; fold the strip over and press as for normal Log Cabin.

9

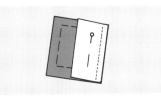

6 Continue around the square clockwise, sewing the smallest strip of Colour 2 (neutral), as shown in diagram 10, then 2 more strips of 1b and 2.

10

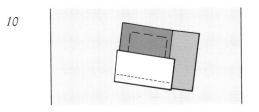

7 Proceed to the next round, which also uses Colours 1b and 2.

8 Sew rounds 3, 4, 5 and 6. As you proceed, trim away excess fabric underneath the strips, leaving allowances of ¼ in/6 mm (see diagram 11). When all the strips have been joined, press the work carefully. Tack around the edge to keep it flat.

11

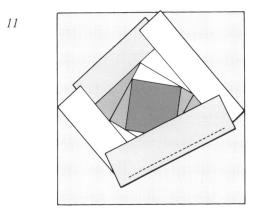

Joining Blocks
1 Stitch the blocks together in the usual way, taking the ½ in/1.2 cm seam allowance. Press the seams open.

2 If paper or Stitch 'n' Tear has been used, carefully tear this away; if interfacing has been used, trim this close to the seam stitching. Trim any excess fabric to leave an even ½ in/1.2 cm seam allowance.

Spiderwebs
and Cobwebs

Sybil Lewis

Until 1980 Sybil Lewis had a full-time career as geography teacher and House Head in a large comprehensive (British secondary) school. Ill health forced her to take early retirement, but a chance introduction to patchwork and quilting "opened up a window", she says, "to a new world of originality and creativity".

She is an active member of the British Quilters' Guild, for whom she has organized workshops and compiled the Guild Directory of Heritage Quilts.

For several years Sybil Lewis taught patchwork and quilting in Adult Education classes, but since 1984 she has concentrated on freelance teaching and lecturing.

Sources and Approaches

Looking at beautiful quilts in the class I attended made me realize that I had found a practical medium for using my enthusiasm for colour and design in an imaginative way. Unfortunately, the chronic arthritis in my hands prevents me from doing fine hand sewing and from carrying out some of the more intricate patchwork techniques. I shall always be grateful to Pauline Burbidge and Sue Simper, who encouraged me to devise and develop my own methods of overcoming this disability while maintaining the high standards of the craft.

It all started with Seminole patchwork, which is always done on the machine, is normally left unquilted and requires no templates. The technique involves joining long strips of fabric to make multicoloured strip-bands, which are then cut across into straight or angled segments and sewn back together in a variety of patterns. The resulting fabric is normally used for clothing and accessories, but my success with this method prompted me to work on a larger scale, producing blocks suitable for quiltmaking. Analysis of traditional blocks showed that many of these patterns could be constructed using these methods.

Research and experiment yielded easier and more efficient methods of cutting and piecing, and as quilting by machine became more widely accepted, I ventured into this field. After working out many variations

Spiderwebs and Stars
(previous page)

Utilizing twenty-four 12 in/30 cm webs devised originally for "Come into My Parlour", but too large for it, I changed the traditional corners. Each web has been turned to stand on a point and the corners squared by adding a specially drafted triangle to each section.

I quilted the main section "in-the-ditch" with an edge-to-edge grid of large squares. This kept the layers together for free machine meandering on the stars. Most of the webs are of random strips except for the top right, which is an example of "Cobweb".

62 × 87 in/158 × 221 cm

Scrap the Blues

A scrap quilt made – in eighteen hours! – to clear my store of some fabrics I disliked. Right-angled triangles cut from random strip-bands were made into squares – a variation of the Spiderweb motif – by seaming pairs along their base line. The work was quilted "in-the-ditch" on the lines of a triangular grid before the mitred border was added. It was then finished with a frame facing.

81 × 58 in/206 × 147 cm

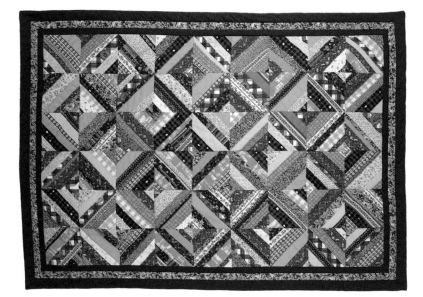

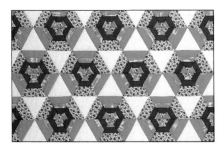

▲ **Hexagonal Spiderwebs**

This quilt, with webs made from strips of different widths, has 4-ounce wadding which limited the quilting to "in-the-ditch". The border is machine-quilted.

92 × 54 in/234 × 137 cm

◄ **Come into My Parlour**

The central lozenge again breaks away from the traditional set, which creates squares where corners meet.

The original template was used for the quilting pattern on the printed background. The rest of the quilting is outline and "in-the-ditch", apart from the free machine meandering on the central background.

73 × 98 in/186 × 250 cm

of strip piecing for myself, I discovered from books that some of these were already known to American quilters, but this has not diminished my own experimentation.

I decided to pass on my findings, not only to the many quilters with problems similar to mine but also to those who wish to piece speedily because of limited leisure time or because of a greater interest in designing or hand quilting.

Almost all of my projects are used as teaching aids to illustrate my methods, so they include a great variety of samples and finished items of clothing, cushions, bags, wallhangings and quilts. The last two are not usually planned as such from the beginning; but if an experiment works well, I continue to make more of the same block or strip-band, laying out the pieces in different ways to see what happens and building up the overall design as I proceed.

Spiderwebs and Cobwebs are traditional names for particular block patterns, but the interpretation of these designs varies. They are very similar to each other. I have made the distinction that a Cobweb is an eight-sectioned block, where every section is made up of the same fabrics in the same sequence. A Spiderweb can have six or eight sections with different fabrics.

I prefer to make quilts and clothes that are practical as well as decorative, so I use fabrics that will tolerate frequent laundering and exposure to sunlight. Having been a compulsive collector of fabrics since the days of wartime rationing, I have an exceptionally large selection from which to choose. A printed fabric of particular interest and colouring will often stimulate ideas for the colour scheme of a patchwork design. The proportion and relationship of each constituent colour within the original print becomes my guide to the selection of compatible fabrics, which may be either plain or patterned. This initial selection may involve many fabrics and hours of deliberation before I achieve a satisfying balance. For me, it is one of the most enjoyable parts of quiltmaking.

Spiderweb Block in Eight Sections

There are several traditional block designs known as Spiderweb or Spider's Web, some of which have other names. Not all of these, however, can be pieced in the manner described in this chapter.

Materials

Assortment of cotton fabrics (see next page)
Drawing and sewing materials (see page 10)

The Seam Allowance

As in all patchwork, the finished effect is dependent on the degree of care and accuracy in all stages of construction. Speed is obtained by using the edge of the presser foot as a stitching guide, *not* by drawing lines on the fabric, and accuracy can be achieved only if the seam made when sewing is exactly the same as the seam allowance included on the templates. Therefore, before drafting the templates it is necessary to check the distance between the needle and the right-hand edge of the presser foot on your machine. If this is not exactly ¼ in/ 6 mm, which is that allowed in the following instructions, you may be able to:

de-centre the needle;
use another foot;
stick a piece of masking tape on the throat plate ¼ in/ 6 mm from the needle.

If none of these remedies is possible, then the seam allowance on the templates must be made the same measurement as that obtained in the initial check of your machine.

Drafting the Templates

There are various methods of drafting the templates for an eight-section Spiderweb block. Two of them are given here. The measurements will produce a block measuring, finished, 12 in/30.5 cm square. For any other size, substitute measurements at *.

Method I

1 Cut a square of very thin but strong paper the actual size required, e.g. 12 in/30.5 cm (*).

2 Fold it diagonally; then fold again 3 times as shown (see diagram 1).

1
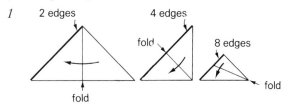

3 Draw along line AB (see diagram 2), made by the final fold.

2
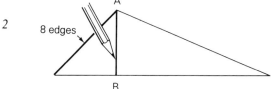

4 Open out the paper; using a ruler, draw the folds marked in black, as in diagram 3.

3
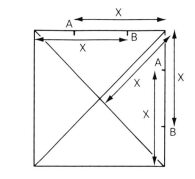

5 Cut out shapes 1 and 2; glue them onto cardboard, add seam allowance, then cut out the cardboard templates.

Note It is not always possible to achieve complete accuracy by this method; however, lines X and Y must be the same measurement. Check your template against the equivalent measurements around the block.

Method II

1 Draw a square of the required size, e.g. 12 in/30.5 cm (*). (The use of squared paper will help to keep the lines straight without lots of measurements and tools.)

2 Find the centre by drawing both diagonals.

3 On the straight edge of a piece of paper, mark off the distance ("X") between one corner and the centre – here 8½ in/21.5 cm (*), as shown in diagram 4.

4 Transfer measurement "X" to the outer edges of the square by marking off from each corner in *both* directions (see diagram 4). Mark these points A and B.

4
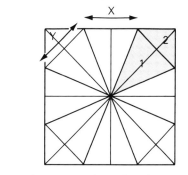

5 Join points A and A and points B and B around the square. Also join the adjacent As and Bs at the corners.

6 Add the usual seam allowances to pieces 1 and 2 (see diagram 5). Glue onto cardboard, then cut out these two templates.

5

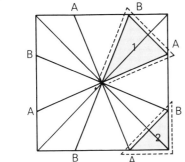

Note A cardboard template is not durable enough to be used as a cutting edge for a rotary cutter, if you wish to use one. To overcome this, stick a piece of masking tape across a large set square to match the size of the cardboard template (see diagram 6). The top edge of the tape now becomes the bottom edge of the original template. Cutting is required only along the long sides of the template. An alternative, now available from Omnigrid, is a 45° Kaleidoscope Wedge Ruler. It is rather expensive but good value if you wish to make lots of Spiderwebs.

6

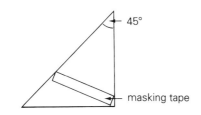

Choice of Fabrics

The colours used for Spiderweb can be contrasting, harmonizing or monochromatic; fabrics can include plains and/or prints. Bear in mind, however, that they should vary in tone and that the corners form the background.

Large prints often give disappointing results with strip piecing, because there is no opportunity to select particular parts of the print for particular patches.

Plaids and stripes that run parallel with the seams tend to emphasize any slight deviation in straight stitching, but they can produce interesting results, especially when used diagonally.

However, extra care is needed when stitching on the bias to prevent stretching.

The Strip-band

1 On the straight grain cut strips as specified below for the two blocks; all strips should be at least 4 times the base of templates (line AB in diagram 5).

For Spiderweb A: (diagram 7a) strips 2 in/5 cm wide from 4 fabrics, adding about 1/8 in/3 mm to the outer strips. (If your Spiderweb is smaller than 12 in/30.5 cm, you will need to adjust the width of the strips; they should total just over half the width/depth of the block, plus seam allowances.)

For Spiderweb B: (diagram 7b) strips of varying widths of 4 or more fabrics, to make the finished band a good 6½ in/16.5 cm wide.

7a 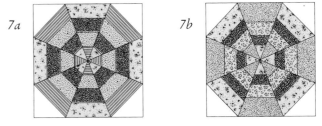 *7b*

2 Set the machine for a medium-fine stitch, and join the strips in a stepped pattern, using the template to obtain the correct angle of slope (see diagram 8). Stepping in this way, although not essential, saves fabric, which could amount to quite a lot in a large quilt. If the inner strips for any strip band are 1 in/2.5 cm or less in width, seam one side as usual, place the next strip underneath, and guide this seam along the *left* edge of the presser foot for the second seam. (For these short lengths it is not necessary to seam in opposite directions; however, this *is* recommended for bands about 55 in/140 cm or more in length – owing to the tendency of fabric to "creep" on most machines.)

8

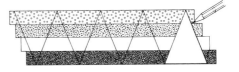

3 Press all seams in the same direction, making sure that there are no pleats on the right side.

4 Using template 1, mark out the cutting lines on the right side, as in diagram 8, making a total of 8 triangles, and cut with scissors or a rotary cutter. If you are using a set square as a template, place the masking tape along the

9

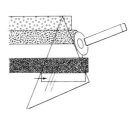

lower edge of the fabric and cut along the sides (see diagram 9) with a rotary cutter.

In either case, to obtain a perfect triangle, it is vital that the seams of the strip-band be kept parallel with the base using lines across the template as a guide both up and down.

Piecing the Web

1 Join each "up" triangle to a "down" triangle (see diagram 10), matching seams if the strips are all the same width. Stitch from the outer edge to the point and just beyond it. Taking a hair's-breadth extra seam allowance for the last third of the seam will prevent the hump that otherwise occurs in the centre where many seams meet. You will find, with practice, that you do *not* need to pin sections together for stitching; however, the point of a long pin placed on the fabric points is useful for keeping them together.

10

2 Join the pairs together, matching the centre seams, to create half webs (see diagram 11). Press all seams on both halves in the same direction (either clockwise or anticlockwise).

11

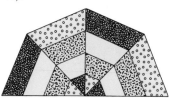

3 Join the two half webs. This time, stitch from the centre outward in both directions: this helps in obtaining an accurate join. Press the work, opening out the seams at the centre.

Adding the Corners

Method I You can cut four triangles from template 2 and join them to the corners in the usual way; however, you may have trouble getting these to fit.

Method II Use any scraps of fabric that are larger than template 2 and have a straight side as long as the base of the triangle. Join them along this side to the four corners (see diagram 12), then mark and trim the outer edges to make a square, using a set square or another right-angled shape as a guide.

12

Spiderweb in Six Sections

A six-section Spiderweb is made up of six equilateral triangles forming a hexagon. The instructions here are for a web measuring 12 in/30 cm across from point to point.

Drafting the Template

Method I Using isometric paper, follow the lines to draw a triangle with 6 in/15 cm sides. Add seam allowance.

Method II Using any paper,

1 Draw a 6 in/15 cm line AB.

2 Place the point of a compass at A, open out the compass until the pencil reaches B (6 in/15 cm) and draw an arc at C.

3 Move the point to B and make another arc crossing the first at C (see diagram 13).

13

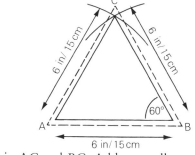

4 Join AC and BC. Add seam allowance all around.

Method III Purchase a 60° triangle grid template for use with a rotary cutter.

Making the Web

1 Make a stepped strip-band 22 in/56 cm long and 6 in/15 cm wide, using 3 strips of fabric.

2 Proceed as for the eight-section Spiderweb, but cut only 6 triangles from the template. When joined, the sections form a hexagonal Spiderweb (see diagram 14).

14

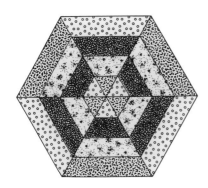

Using Hexagonal Spiderwebs

Whereas eight-section Spiderweb blocks, being square, can easily be joined to make a quilt – either edge-to-edge or with alternating plain blocks or sashing (see page 12) – hexagonal blocks must be joined with additional contrasting triangles, so that the webs will be readily visible. These are cut exactly the same size as the other triangles and are joined to opposite sides of each hexagon. The diamonds are then joined into vertical rows (see diagram 15) and the rows joined to make the complete patchwork. Half webs and half triangles must be added at each end to make them square.

15

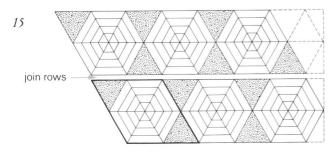

join rows

Spiderweb Quilt

If all the hexagonal webs are to be identical, construct long strip-bands in multiples of 7 in+/18 cm+ (assuming a block with 6 in/15 cm sides). For example, a stepped band 36 in/92 cm long will give 5 "up" triangles and 5 "downs"; a band 45 in/115 cm long will give 6 "up" triangles and 6 "downs".

1 Make 28 webs from 18 strip-bands, each measuring 36 in/92 cm long and 6 in+/15 cm+ wide.

2 For each web cut 2 more from the original template of background fabric. Stitch these to two opposite edges of the web, making a diamond.

3 Join the diamonds in vertical rows (see diagram 15), making 3 rows of 6 webs and 2 rows of 5.

4 Make a new template for half-triangles by dividing a 6 in/15 cm triangle in half down the centre and adding

seam allowance. Cut 4 "ups" and 4 "downs" from the strip-band and 12 from background fabric. Also make 8 full-size triangles, 4 "up" and 4 "down" from the strip-band. Make up 4 half-webs.

5 Join half-webs and half-triangles, as required, to the rows to make the ends square. Then join the rows to make the complete quilt top.

6 Machine quilt before the border is added, but add the border before hand quilting.

Cobweb

Also sometimes referred to as Spider's Web, this block is made of sections in which the arrangement of strips is uniform, rather than alternating. It is constructed in exactly the same manner as the eight-section Spiderweb, but if the outer and inner fabrics are to be different, as in diagram 16, you will need twice the usual length of strip-band, accommodating 8 triangles on a side. If you are making many webs (for a quilt, for example), you can cut 8 "up" and 8 "down" triangles, and use these for two different, contrasting webs.

16

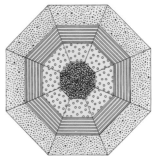

An alternative, if identical cobwebs are required, is to make a strip-band consisting of an odd number of strips which are identical in width and fabric on each side of the centre strip. The triangles are then cut alternately up and down and joined to form a web, as shown in diagram 17.

17

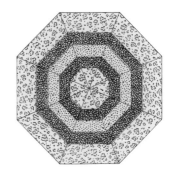

Cathedral Window

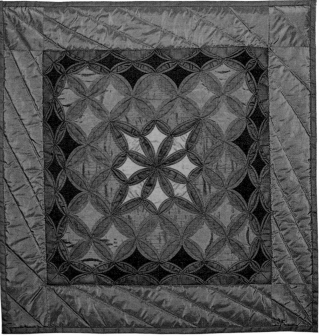

Lynne Edwards

An enthusiastic teacher and dedicated needleworker, Lynne Edwards has made quilts for twenty years, and her work is now shown in galleries and exhibitions. It is almost entirely hand stitched. Since the late 1980s she has concentrated on the technique of Cathedral Window and has created many spectacular variations on this theme.

Sources and Approaches

It was while training as a junior school teacher that I became interested in crafts, and in dressmaking in particular. I soon discovered the pleasure of browsing through fabric departments; it was (and still is) a great delight to see the bolts of fabric lined up next to each other, especially the printed Liberty lawns, with each design challenging its neighbour. In the adventurous spirit of the '60s I sometimes used two or three different prints in one dress.

From there it was a short step to discovering patchwork. Earlier, I had already dabbled in a little hexagon patchwork, but it was unplanned, uninspiring and unfinished. A visit to the American Museum in Bath opened my eyes to what a quilt could be. I gathered up my collection of delectable fabric bits and set to work.

That was twenty years ago, and since then I have read, studied techniques, experimented and above all sewn constantly. My interest in Cathedral Window was stimulated through making a small sample while on a course some twelve years ago. It consisted of just four basic folded squares in one colour with contrasting overlaid windows, but the design possibilities of the form were apparent even then. I soon discovered that a very subtle effect could be achieved by changing the colour of the background squares, sewing one folded square to another of a different fabric. The checkerboard effect seems very obvious when the squares are first sewn together, but definitions are blurred when the windows are sewn in position, as these lie across the joined squares, obscuring the changes from one colour to the next.

All my work now is based on creating subtlety of colour and movement using Cathedral Window and its variation, known as Secret Garden. I no longer limit the shape of the folded background to one size of square, but am experimenting with rectangles, triangles and smaller and larger squares within the same piece. This creates movement more dynamically than I had thought possible.

Kingfisher Blue Hanging
(previous page)

Having mastered various rectangular shapes as the basis for Cathedral Window, I wanted to see if a triangular shape was possible. After some struggles and many complex mathematical calculations, I found that, although not simple, it was possible. Using this shape, plus squares and rectangles, I designed a block to be used in the same way as the classic patchwork blocks – repeated in a quilt, with lattice strips between, or several used in a group to make an overall design. This hanging is made from four blocks, joined with the triangular areas all at the centre. I intend to exploit the block in future designs and explore its possibilities in different ways.

27½ × 27½ in/70 × 70 cm

▼ **Yellow Silk Wallhanging**

A symmetrical central area of Cathedral Window with half-opened Secret Garden in the corners. Striped fabrics have been used for both background and windows, providing many nuances of colour and pattern.

32½ × 32½ in/82 × 82 cm

Silver-Blue Tower Wallhanging
(overleaf)

I love the subtle colour effects that can be created by using background squares of different fabrics and then concealing the joins with the overlying window. There are no sudden changes where two fabrics meet, the colours flow into each other. The Tower itself is constructed of many different Cathedral Window squares and overlying windows. The background is of Secret Garden, with one part only opened out.

24 × 31½ in/60 × 80 cm

Green Distorted Tower ▶

In this tower, I have tried to achieve a strong flow from the darker focus upwards in long sweeping curves. The background to the tower is Secret Garden, using a series of rectangular and square shapes to link with the shapes in the Cathedral Window Tower itself.

22 × 35½ in/55 × 90 cm

◀ Silver Birch Wallhanging

Having experimented with extended blocks, I wanted to make a large piece that was very balanced and kaleidoscopic. Although the windows are irregular in shape, the overall effect is still formal and symmetrical. I had planned to take the design right out to the corners of the piece but found that it just would not be taken any farther. Instead, the four corner areas are plain fabric, which I then hand-quilted.

53 × 53 in/135 × 135 cm

The ideas always develop from the fabric. I especially like to use silk, at least for the windows, because of the quality of light it brings to the work. I walk around the fabrics for days, deciding which should be used. These now are seldom prints, but I do enjoy the effect that a striped fabric can produce. The decision on fabrics is followed by lots of vague sketching and, in turn, by a more accurate drawing to establish the block shapes needed for the design. These are strictly working diagrams, and I shade in pencil rather than colour, adding scribbled notes as to what fabric is to be used where. I like to keep the design open-ended, and I often alter the colours as I go along. In that way the excitement and exploration are continuous throughout the work.

Moving into expensive and less practical fabrics like silk has meant that I now make few bed quilts, usually only for special commissions. I find that making smaller pieces allows me to explore ideas and colour changes more quickly and develop these into a series without losing the excitement.

Hung on a wall, the quilt can be appreciated like a painting, revealing different aspects of itself as the light changes. Like a good picture, it should always offer something new to the observer, no matter how many times he or she has looked at it.

▼ **Cathedral Window – Movement**

Changing shapes in Cathedral Window can accentuate the flowing qualities of shifts of colour. I tried in this piece to make a focus in the lower left-hand quarter with the strongest colour and then to move out from it in curving lines, with the colours gradually fading in intensity. Some of these blocks are very eccentric in shape and use a large amount of fabric, so for economy I used polished cotton as the base shapes, restricting silk to the windows.

35½ × 35½ in/90 × 90 cm

Basic Cathedral Window

The first point to make is that fabric is not like paper: it moves, it distorts, it shrinks in one direction when you press it and not in the other. No wonder it will not make a perfect flat envelope shape every time. The golden rule is: always blame the fabric, never yourself. Once the waywardness of fabric has been acknowledged, it is easier to beat it into submission.

Suitable Fabrics
Any firm, medium-weight fabric, preferably made of natural fibres, is ideal. A flimsy or slippery fabric can be made firmer with spray starch before any folding or cutting begins. Always test first in case of water marks. Either plain or patterned fabric can be used: striped fabric can be very effective. Although traditionally only one fabric is used for the basic folded squares, there is no reason why several different fabrics should not be used, both for the base squares and for the smaller windows that are laid on top of the background.

Method of Construction
The smallest unit of Cathedral Window requires two folded squares of base fabric, plus one smaller square for the window.

1 Cut two 8 in/20 cm squares of the main fabric by drawing around a cardboard template.

2 Fix the centre of each base square by folding diagonally and pressing lightly first one way and then the other, using the point of the iron. (A steam iron is ideal for this technique; alternatively use a separate spray-on water bottle with a dry iron.)

3 Unfold each square; with the wrong side of the fabric uppermost, turn in each edge ¼ in/6 mm and press firmly. Do this by eye and by running the steam iron along each edge as you fold it (see diagram 1).

1

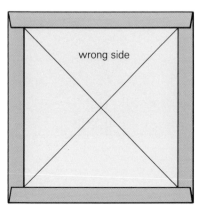

4 Fold each corner exactly into the centre, where they should meet. Each outside corner should be sharp-pointed. Press well (see diagram 2). At this point, things sometimes start to look wrong. If this happens, press the square back to its original flat shape with the ¼ in/6 mm turning and begin again. First take one corner to the centre and press lightly. Now take the next corner into the centre. If they fail to meet and one seems much longer than the other (as in diagram 3), adjust them so that they are level with each other and the outer point is as sharp as possible. If this means that the centre corners do not lie exactly on the marked mid-point, or even overlap each other, do not worry. The important thing is to get the outside corners very sharp and well pressed.

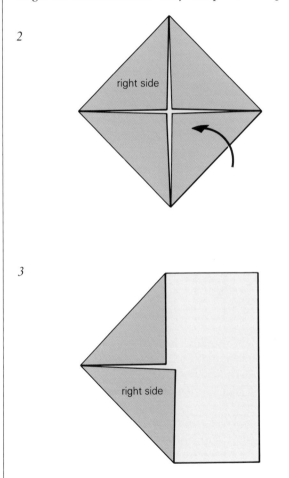

5 If the centre points are not lying in a cross shape (as in diagram 2), adjust them, even if this means that the envelope shape no longer lies flat. Secure the centre points by working two or three tiny stitches through all the layers, starting and finishing at the back, where the thread can be left ready for use. Press each of the four corners again. Do not expect necessarily to be able to run the iron over the whole envelope, as it may well be uneven.

6 Bring the four corners again to the centre, still keeping them as sharp as possible. Any excess fabric within the shape can be lost in the folded area as the corners are brought to the middle. Using the original thread, sew the centre down firmly through all layers (diagram 4). Fasten off at the back of the work. The four outside corners can be made sharper if necessary by pinching them into shape and pressing. The square should now measure a little over 3¾ in/9.5 cm.

4

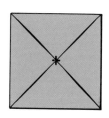

7 When both squares have been prepared in this way, place them together with folded sides facing, and oversew them together along one edge with tiny stitches. Open out again.

8 Cut a small contrasting fabric square to measure 2⅜ in/6 cm. Place it over the centre square formed across the joined envelope shapes. Trim it down if necessary until a border of about ⅛ in/3 mm shows all around. Pin it in position (see diagram 5).

5

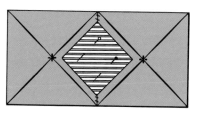

9 Roll the surrounding border over the edge of the contrasting square and sew it down onto the square with tiny spaced back stitches, worked close to the edge, stretching the edge (which is on the bias) into a curved shape as you go. Continue around all four sides. At the corners secure the contrasting fabric well with a double bar stitch (2 superimposed stitches) at least ¼ in/6 mm down from the corner (see diagram 6).

6

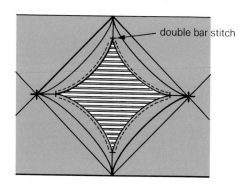

double bar stitch

10 This is the basic Cathedral Window. As more folded squares are joined together, more windows can be applied (see diagram 7).

7

Secret Garden Variation

This requires only one 8 in/20 cm square of fabric, plus a contrasting square measuring 3¾ in/9.5 cm.

1 Proceed as for Cathedral Window, steps 2–5, pressing ¼ in/6 mm on each edge, folding each corner into the centre and fastening them down firmly with a few small stitches. (You have now folded the corners in only once.)

2 Bring the four corners into the centre. Again, they should meet exactly, and the outer corners should be sharp. Press well and then unfold again. The fold lines should be clearly visible (see diagram 8).

8

3 Lay the contrasting square on top of the larger square, using the fold lines as a guide for positioning. If necessary, trim the contrasting square slightly, so that the fold lines are just visible outside it. Sew the square in place, using a small running stitch through all the layers about ⅛ in/3 mm from the edge (see diagram 9).

9

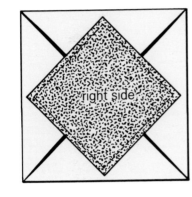

right side

4   Bring the four outer corners over the contrasting square to the centre and press. Follow the instructions for Cathedral Window to achieve sharp corners and sew these down firmly.

5   The bias edges are now rolled back to reveal the contrasting square and sewn down with a series of tiny backstitches, as for Cathedral Window. Do not turn the edges back right up to the outer corners, as this would reveal the raw edge of the contrasting fabric beneath. Instead, place a pin through all layers about ¼ in/6 mm in from the corner. Working from the centre, turn the edges back up to this point, then remove the pin and secure the edges with a double bar stitch across them, worked through all the layers, before continuing sewing. Do this in each corner (diagram 10). A four-pointed flower shape is now revealed beneath the bias edges.

10

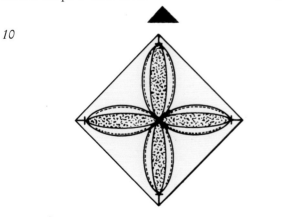

6   Individual blocks may be joined by placing them together with right sides facing and oversewing the edges neatly.

Expanded Blocks

The process of making an expanded block is quite different from making an ordinary square one. A paper pattern is used, and this is drawn by graphically reversing the folding procedure.

Drafting the Template

1   Start by drawing the final shape of one of the envelopes, full size, on graph paper (see diagram 11a). Indicate the folded edges of the piece meeting in the centre with 2 diagonal lines.

11a

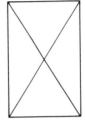

2   Draw the same rectangle in pencil, omitting the inner folds; then draw a horizontal and a vertical line through the middle of the rectangle, extending them some distance outside it. Measure the distance from Z to A (see diagram 11b). Mark a point X on the upper half of the vertical line, so that AX equals ZA. Do the same for ZB/BY; ZC/CW; ZD/DV. Connect the points now labelled W, X, Y and Z, with 4 diagonal lines touching the corners of the rectangle to form a diamond (see diagram 11b).

11b

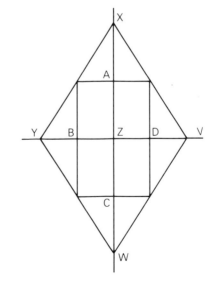

3 Make a tracing of one triangular quarter of the diamond (here labelled X, Y, Z). Draw the diamond shape in pencil. Trace around the triangle on each side of the diamond. This forms the complete shape (see diagram 11c). Add ¼ in/6 mm seam allowance all round. Cut out this shape and glue it onto cardboard to make the template.

11c

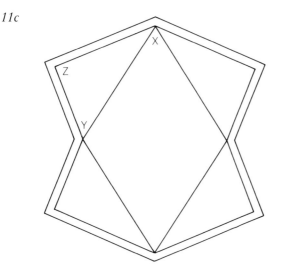

4 For the window template(s), trace the four-sided shape formed over two adjoining envelopes which can be symmetrical or asymmetrical (see diagram 12).

The shape cut from this template can be folded into the required original envelope shape only by using a special machine-stitched technique.

12

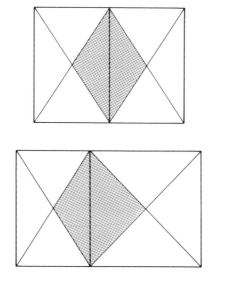

Constructing the Block

1 Draw around the cardboard template on the wrong side of the fabric, and cut out the shape.

2 Fold the fabric piece in half, right sides together, along line AB (see diagram 13). Machine stitch the shorter edges together as shown (diagram 14). Open out the shape, and fold from C to D so that the seams are aligned. Machine stitch from C to about 1 in/2.5 cm from the centre, leaving a long length of double threads at C. Repeat from D to 1 in/2.5 cm from the centre (see diagram 15).

13

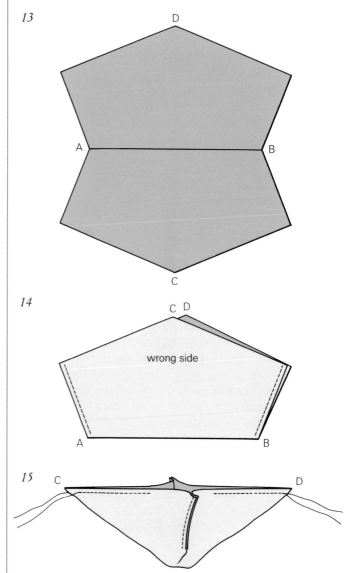

14

15

3 Trim the corners diagonally at C and D. Press the four seams open, then turn the envelope right side out. To pull out the long corners at C and D, thread a needle with the machine threads at C and re-insert it in the fabric as near the edge of the fold as possible. Holding the needle, pull the corner through to the right side. Repeat at D; trim off threads. Press. Sew the centre edges together with two or three tiny stitches through all the layers. Fold and press the corners to the centre, and secure them as for basic Cathedral Window.

Wallhanging

Shades of pink and grey silk have been used for the windows and border of this wallhanging. The background is of polished cotton. Blocks of Secret Garden around the edges heighten the impact of the expanded blocks in the centre of the design. The hanging measures approximately 35½ in/90 cm square.

Materials

For background, 4 fabrics, 45 in/115 cm wide: fabric A, 1⅛ yards/1 metre; fabric B, ¾ yard/70 cm; fabric C, 1 yard/90 cm; fabric D, ¾ yard/70 cm
For windows, 4 assorted silk fabrics, any width:
    ¼ yard/20 cm of each
For border, silk to harmonize with fabric D, any width:
    ½ yard/50 cm
For backing, suitable fabric, any width:
    1 yard/90 cm
For binding, piece of fabric A from quantity above
Wadding (lightweight – 2-ounce): ½ yard/50 cm
Drawing and sewing materials (see page 10)

Patchwork

1   Cut the following templates:
X: 6½ in/16.5 cm square (for 3 in/7.5 cm envelope)
Y: 9½ in/24 cm square (for 4½ in/11.5 cm envelope)
Z: template traced from diagram 16 (for rectangular envelope 3 × 4½ in/7.5 × 11.5 cm)
5 window templates traced from diagram 17

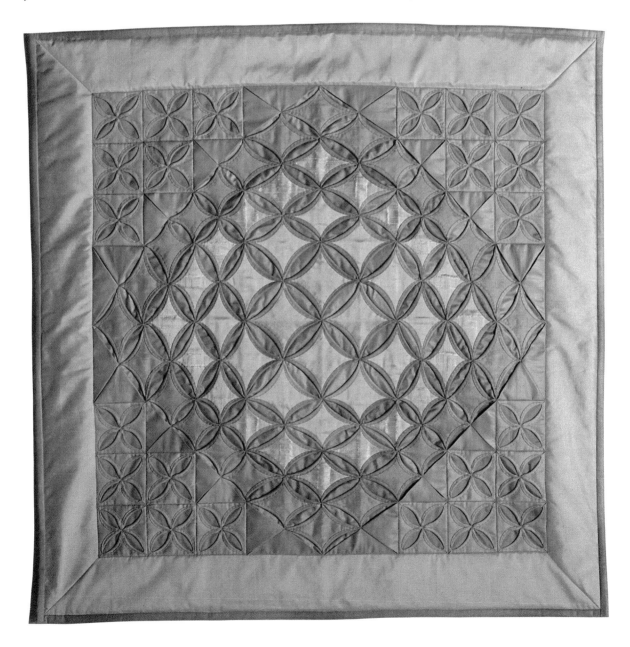

16   *17*

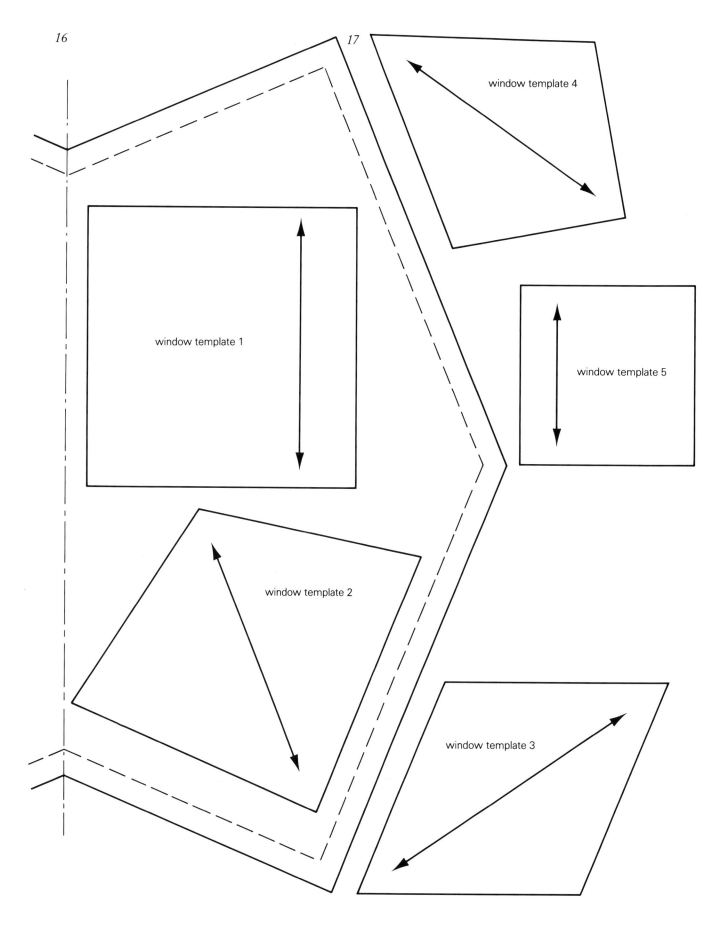

window template 4

window template 1

window template 5

window template 2

window template 3

18

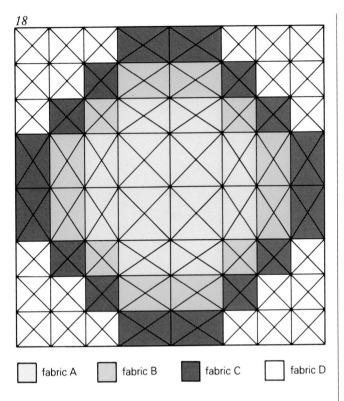

| ☐ fabric A | ☐ fabric B | ■ fabric C | ☐ fabric D |

19

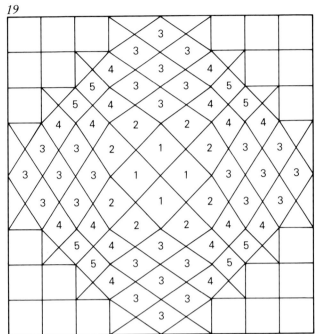

In constructing the patchwork, follow diagram 18 for background blocks and colours, diagram 19 for positions of window templates.

2   From fabric A, cut and sew 4 squares of "Y" size and 8 rectangles of "Z" size. Join the four squares together to make one large square. Using window Template (1), cut 4 windows from chosen silk fabric. Pin and sew these in position, taking care to keep the grain in the same direction, otherwise the colour will not appear to be the same.

3   Join the 8 rectangles to each square (see diagram 18). These will now make places for 8 windows using Template (2) and 4 windows using Template (3). Use the same fabric for these windows as for the square ones, keeping the direction of the grain constant.

4   From fabric B, cut and construct 8 rectangles and 4 smaller squares ("X" size). Join these around the edges of the fabric A section. Cut and sew on 12 windows from Template (3) and 8 windows from Template (4), using another shade of fabric.

5   In the same way, add 8 rectangles and 8 smaller squares, all in fabric C, around the edges of the work. Using a third silk fabric, cut and sew on 12 windows from Template (3), 8 from Template (4) and 8 from Template (5).

6   Fill in each corner with 6 Secret Garden blocks made from the "X" size, using fabric D. The window for these should be a 3 in/7.5 cm square.

Border

1   For the border cut 4 strips of fabric, each 4 × 35 in/10 × 89 cm and 4 strips of wadding the same size. Cut the backing to measure 35 in/89 cm square. For the binding cut 4 strips of fabric A, each 2 × 36 in/5 × 92 cm.

2   Pin a strip of wadding under each border strip of fabric. Machine a line of stitches ¼ in/6 mm in from one long edge of the fabric and wadding. Trim the wadding from the seam allowance close to the stitching. Press the seam allowance over the wadding, folding the fabric exactly along the line of the stitching.

3   Placing right sides together, and leaving 4 in/10 cm of border extending beyond the patchwork at each end, oversew the folded edge of the border to the edge of the patchwork with small stitches. Following the diagonal line of the blocks, fold under and press each loose end of the border to form mitred corners. Pin and sew the ends together through all layers along the folded lines; trim back the wadding close to the mitred seams, trim the extra fabric to a ¼ in/6 mm seam allowance and press.

4   Pin or tack the backing fabric to the piece and secure by tying at regular intervals with sewing thread and knotting at the back. Use the strips of fabric A to bind the edges of the completed hanging (see page 17).

Three-Dimensional Patchwork

Jennie Rayment

Since the mid-1970s Jennie Rayment has been involved with sewing in one form or another, running her own business (producing needlecraft items) and developing her skills by attending courses on many different aspects of needlework. Having obtained a teaching diploma, she discovered the great satisfaction of sharing her knowledge with others; she is now a tutor in Adult Education for two county authorities and also conducts private classes and workshops.

Sources and Approaches

I try not to specialize in any single area of patchwork, quilting or appliqué and would describe myself as an adult addicted to play. It is through playing that many different ideas and designs develop. I like to experiment with shape, image and methods of construction. To work in the traditional manner is excellent, but in my view it is worthwhile trying new techniques and alternative ways to produce interesting pieces. Even when this is unsuccessful, it is a valuable exercise in opening the mind to new creative possibilities.

Geometric design has tremendous appeal to most patchworkers; in Britain the most used geometric shape is the hexagon. We have all used hexagons at some point in our piecing career, stitching them together in their hundreds to form quilts, wallhangings, pincushions and many other items, only to realize that there is a limit to the designs that can be achieved using the shape in its two-dimensional form.

However, it is from the lowly hexagon that three-dimensional patchwork springs. By dissecting this simple shape and altering its proportions, many optical illusions can be created. Some patterns develop from a simple diamond, while others use a combination of diamonds and squares. It is fascinating to expand the basic form and see a multitude of exciting images emerge. The geometric shapes leap into life and take on a force of their own, having a depth and substance not usually found in other patchwork blocks.

Stalk Eyes
(previous page)

Named by my husband as he sees eyes on stalks in the design! Machine pieced and quilted throughout, it was developed from Roman mosaic floors in Turkey.

41 × 41 in/104 × 104 cm

◄ **Steps in Time**

This wallhanging has been hand pieced, then completed with machine and hand quilting.

56 × 60 in/142 × 152 cm

Turquoise Tumbling Blocks ▶

The central tumbling blocks design on this cushion has been machine pieced, then hand applied to the curved strip background.

16 × 16 in/40.5 × 40.5 cm

▼ **Marooned**

This wallhanging has an additional three-dimensional effect created with a folded bias strip around the centre and with piping round the individual blocks. The inspiration for the idea came through playing with the shapes. It is machine pieced, hand applied and quilted both by hand and by machine.

22 × 38 in/55 × 97 cm

Playing with hexagons is not unique to patchwork; these versatile shapes appear – both whole and subdivided into diamond shapes – in the decorative arts of many ancient cultures. The Romans, for instance, used hexagonal designs in their mosaics. There is an excellent example of Tumbling Blocks at the Temple of Apollo in Pompeii and on the floor of the Villa of the Volussi, at Lucius Feroniae in Rome. Other examples can be seen at Fishbourne and Bignor, near Chichester, Sussex.

In some Italian churches and palaces, particularly in Venice, there are fine marble floors displaying imaginative uses of three-dimensional shapes. The motif known in patchwork as Trefoil or Inner City occurs in many of the ecclesiastical buildings, and although this is formed by bisecting the hexagon, there is still a visual illusion. It is well worth taking a camera when travelling, for visual inspiration can be found in many unusual places.

Tumbling blocks in their familiar form did not appear in English patchwork until the nineteenth century, although examples of hexagons, or honeycomb as it is sometimes called, can be found in quilts and wallhangings from 1700 onwards. It was the Victorians who developed the Tumbling or Baby Block to great effect, using an assortment of different fabrics to suggest a three-dimensional image. This "box pattern", as it was often termed, has remained to this day. Three-dimensional effects are achieved by dividing a hexagon into three component parts, the visual deception arising through the use of colour, tone and (sometimes) texture. The enormous variety of designs that can be achieved is suggested by the photographs on these pages.

Construction of a Three-Dimensional Block

Materials

Selection of fabric: solid colours and small prints in a good range of tones

Drawing and sewing materials (see page 10), including a protractor

The designs on the previous page are formed from two kinds of hexagon: regular and irregular (see diagram 1).

A regular hexagon is composed of six equal sides and can be divided into three equal sections – diamonds. This division produces the design known as Tumbling or Baby Blocks.

An irregular hexagon (lozenge shape) is also composed of six equal sides, but the angles are different from those in the regular hexagon. This can be divided into three sections – two equal diamonds plus a square.

1

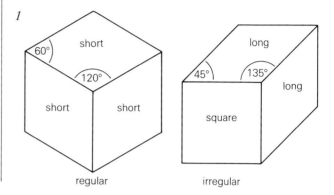

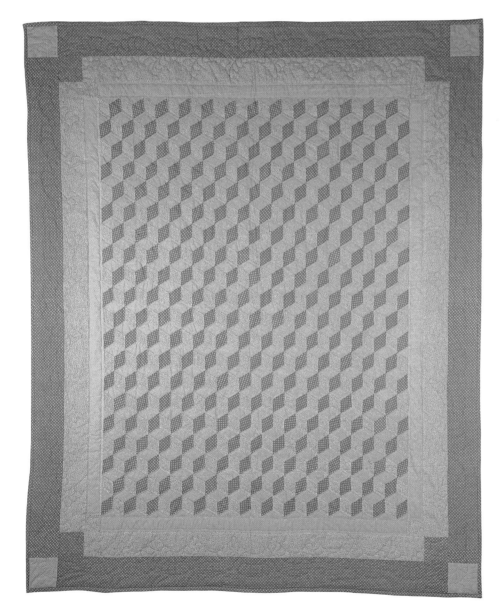

◀ **Yellow and Blue Tumbling Blocks**

Created by Jean McNeill, this is her first quilt and the colours have been chosen to match an existing decor. It is hand and machine pieced, then quilted completely by hand.

96 × 96 in/244 × 244 cm

Before attempting to construct a three-dimensional block, it is necessary to understand the basic difference between the two hexagons. The regular one breaks down into three equal-sided diamonds with internal angles of 60° and 120°. These are often referred to as "short diamonds".

The irregular hexagon is composed of two equal-sized diamonds plus a square. The angles within the diamonds are 45° and 135° respectively, and are often referred to as "long diamonds".

Short diamonds and long diamonds will not fit together, nor will the square shape fit into a block with short diamonds (see diagram 2). Therefore designs need to be analyzed to distinguish between the two types.

2

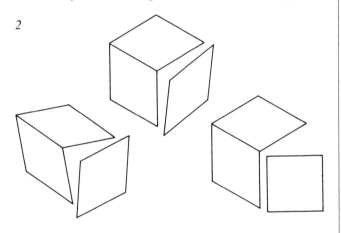

Drafting the Templates

You can buy hexagon templates in various sizes, or construct one with a compass, by drawing a circle, marking the radius 6 times around the circumference and then joining up the points. However, I prefer to use a protractor, since this enables me to develop many variations of the basic shape.

Regular Hexagon The three diamonds required for this are constructed as follows (see diagram 3):

Method A
1 Rule and mark line AB, the finished length of one side of the diamond; here it is 2 in/5 cm.

2 Place the protractor on point B, lining up the centre of the protractor with B; measure 60°, using the outer ring of numbers (diagram 3a).

3a

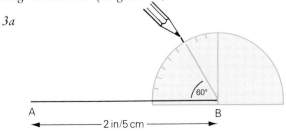

3 Move the protractor to point A, lining up the centre of the protractor with A; measure 60°, using the outer ring of numbers (diagram 3b).

3b

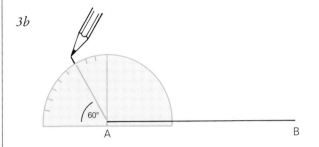

4 Rule a line from point B through the 60° mark, the same length as AB, to point C.

5 Repeat with a line from point A through the 60° mark, again the same length as AB, to point D (diagram 3c).

3c

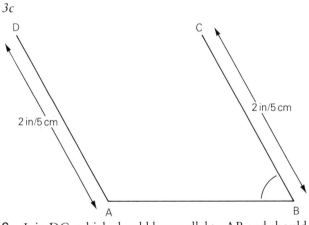

6 Join DC, which should be parallel to AB and should measure the same as the other sides.

Three of these diamonds joined together will make a 4 in/10 cm Tumbling Block (see diagram 4).

4

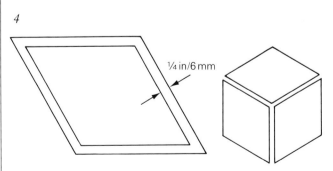

7 Cut out the shape and glue it onto thin cardboard; add a seam allowance of ¼ in/6 mm all around (see diagram 4). If you are using the English method of piecing (see page 101), you will also need a template of the shape *without* seam allowances.

Irregular Hexagon (see diagram 5)

1 Construct a square of the required size; here it is 2 in/5 cm. Mark the four corners A, B, C and D, starting at the top left and going in a clockwise direction. (Using graph paper will make this easy; otherwise mark 90° angles with the protractor.)

2 Place the protractor on point A, lining up its centre with A, and measure 45°, using the outer ring of numbers (see diagram 5a).

5a

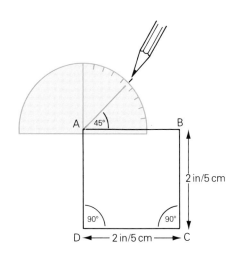

3 Move the protractor to point B, lining up its centre with B, and measure 45°, using the outer ring of numbers (see diagram 5b).

5b

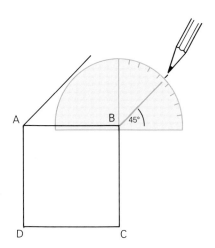

4 Rule a line from point A through the 45° mark, measuring the same length as AB, to point X.

5 Repeat with a line from point B through the 45° mark, again the same length as AB, to point Y (see diagram 5c).

5c

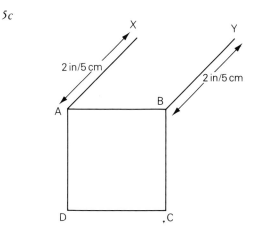

6 Join XY, which should be parallel to AB and measure the same length. If not, it is wrong somewhere!

7 To complete the hexagon, measure a 45° angle at point C and rule a line through the mark to point Z, the same length as the other lines; finally, join points Y and Z (see diagram 5d). This hexagon measures, finished, 4⅞ in/12.5 cm long (between D and Y) and 2⅞ in/7.3 cm wide (between A and C).

5d

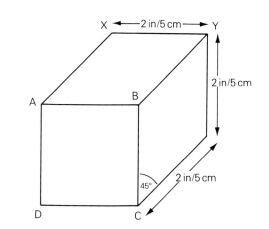

8 For templates, cut out the square and just one of the diamonds; glue these onto cardboard and add ¼ in/6 mm seam allowance.

Choosing the Fabrics

Whichever type of three-dimensional patchwork you choose to make, colour and tone are vital. The three-dimensional effect is the result of our perceiving the shapes as illuminated by an unseen light source, which strikes some planes of the blocks, leaving others in different degrees of shadow (see diagram 6). If one colour range is being used, choose light, medium and dark tones to create the illusion. If three different colours are to be used they should vary sufficiently in tone to achieve the same effect.

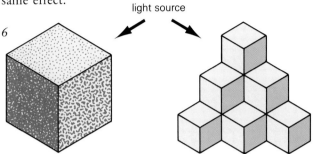

light source

6

Large, busy prints do not lend themselves to this type of patchwork because they tend to detract from the geometric effect. Look at directional fabrics to see if stripes can be used to enhance further the three-dimensional appearance, but do watch the cutting out, and make sure you lay the template in the right direction! Texture, too, can be exploited for this purpose. For example, lines of pin tucks in different directions will create soft contrasts. Experiment with changing the colours within the blocks to diffuse the light source. Be creative and play. With so little fabric involved, the sense of achievement far outweighs the cost of mistakes.

Piecing Tumbling Blocks

There are two methods of piecing the blocks. One is the English method, worked over pieces of paper. This is somewhat time consuming, but many people prefer it. The American method is faster and involves no cutting of papers; it can be very successful provided you are able to sew straight and maintain an even seam allowance.

Whichever method you choose, two opposite sides of the template should be aligned with the straight grain of the fabric (see diagram 7a), unless it has a directional design that you wish to exploit. If you place the diamond with all four sides on the bias (diagram 7b) there is a greater chance of distortion in the completed work.

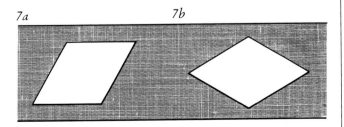

7a   7b

Basic English method

1   Using the basic shape (without seam allowances) as a template, cut the required number of paper shapes for your design.

2   Use the template with seam allowances to cut out fabrics, or pin the paper templates to the fabric, leaving room to cut ¼ in/6 mm around the shape (diagram 8).

8

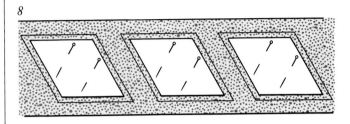

3   Tack the fabric shapes to the papers, folding corners carefully (diagram 9).

9

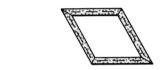

4   Oversew pieces together with small, firm stitches. Sew into the Tumbling Block first (diagram 10), join the blocks in the same way. When the patchwork is complete, remove the papers.

10

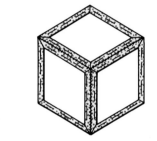

American Method

Accuracy is essential in both cutting out and sewing. I prepare a template, including the seam allowances, using the plastic sheeting available, and with a pencil I trace around the diamond shape onto the fabric. Then I very carefully cut out on the pencil lines.

1   By layering the fabrics or folding one piece into four, you can cut out several diamonds at once with a rotary cutter (but watch your fingers!). If you prefer to draw around the shape, make sure to draw on the wrong side of the fabric, and hold the pencil point at an angle of 45° to the surface to get really close to the shape. Cut just *inside* the pencil line, because the line was drawn *outside* the template. This will give the correct size.

2   When all the pieces are cut out, lay them out and check that the three-dimensional illusion is apparent. Try viewing the patchwork from all sides to see the differing effects.

Hand-stitched Tumbling Blocks

Seam allowances should be ¼ in/6 mm. If you prefer to use a different seam allowance do make sure that it remains constant. Decreasing or increasing the seam allowance measurement from that specified in a project will alter the size of the end product.

Whether the work is stitched by hand or machine, the American method assumes the existence of an imaginary dot ¼ in/6 mm from the end of the central seam. The dot must also be taken into account when stitching the blocks together. The fabrics can twist around, as their seam allowances are free. This is the secret of successful piecing (see diagram 11a).

11a

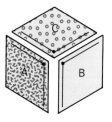

1 Placing right sides together, join diamond pieces A and B, using either backstitch or a combination of 2 to 3 running stitches followed by a backstitch. This second method works well. Sew from the base of the block to ¼ in/6 mm from the centre (see diagram 11b). There is no need to break the thread.

11b

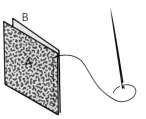

2 Open out the shapes. Place the third diamond, C, against A, with right sides and raw edges matching. Make a firm backstitch at the join, and continue sewing to the end (diagram 11c). Fasten off.

3 Re-form the block, and stitch from the mid-point to the end of the seam (diagram 11d).

11c   *11d*

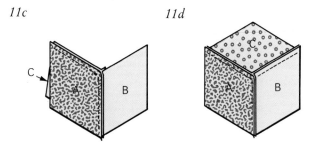

Machine-stitched Tumbling Blocks

1 Lay out the pieces in block form (see diagram 12a). It is best to sew one block at a time, as it is very easy to stitch wrong sections together.

12a

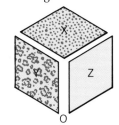

2 Join pieces Y and Z, and stitch from point (O) to ¼ in/6 mm from the top of the seam. Fasten off.

3 Open out the shape. Place diamond X next to Y, taking care to line them up exactly. Sew from one end to the centre, finishing where the first stitching ended (diagram 12b). Fasten off.

12b

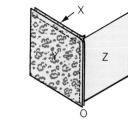

4 Open out the shapes and swing the third section around to match Z. Reverse the work and stitch to the centre, matching the seams exactly. Open out the block and press. Make sure that all stitching finishes at the central point, or the block will not lie flat.

If you find a little hole in the centre, either the stitching lines have not been close enough or the stitch length is slightly too big. Close the seam by hand, stitching carefully.

Assembly of Pieces – American Method

1 Arrange the blocks in your design. Stitch them together in rows, either by hand or by machine, leaving a ¼ in/6 mm gap at each end of the seam, taking great care not to catch in any seam allowances (see diagram 13).

The crucial factor in assembling by hand or machine is to make sure that ¼ in/6 mm is left at both ends of every seam and that no seam allowances are caught.

13

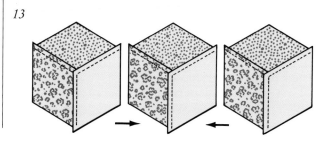

2 The rows can be assembled on the machine, using the same principle, but it is probably less stressful to join them by hand (see diagram 14). Take great care to stitch firmly at the junction of six seams (diagram 15). A helpful tip is to run the needle through all the points and backstitch firmly before proceeding.

14

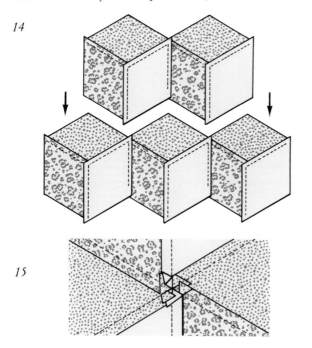

15

3 Press the work well on the wrong side. The seams will lie in all directions. I have found it is best to press them to one side, away from the light fabrics. At the junctions of many seams I place the point of the iron right at the centre; this will usually fan out the points to make the work flatter.

Piecing an Irregular Hexagon
Either the English or the American method can be used to piece these blocks. With the American method, the imaginary ¼ in/6 mm point is still of vital importance and you may find it helpful to mark the fabric with a dot at this point (see diagram 16). Join the diamonds first, then add the square.

Because this shape has a distinct bias in one direction, do cut out the diamonds carefully, particularly if you are using a striped or one-way fabric.

16

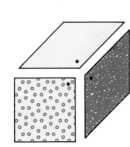

Completing the Patchwork
A design of Tumbling Blocks could be appliquéd onto a background fabric. Select a fabric that will enhance the patchwork and provide sufficient contrast to it. When applying the patchwork to the background, turn down the seam allowance all around the edges and press well; tack if necessary. Pin and tack the work to the background, making sure that the edges and internal lines are parallel where necessary. Use the normal blind appliqué stitch (slipstitch), and keep the stitches as small as possible, pulling the thread firmly.

If you wish to use the piece in a square or rectangular area, it is preferable to make it larger than the area to be filled, rather than trying to fill gaps around the edges with half or quarter blocks, which is a tricky operation and likely to produce work that refuses to lie flat.

Exploring the Three-dimensional Concept
Having learned how to construct blocks and stitch them together, you can now begin to experiment with them to produce complete designs.

1 Purchase some isometric paper (which saves drawing countless tumbling blocks), and shade in different sections to produce a variety of three-dimensional effects. Cut the pieces out and move them around in as many combinations as you can think of.

2 When drawing either of the two basic hexagons, elongate the sides to distort the design. Many different optical illusions can emerge, particularly when the light sources are changed.

3 Utilize the square in the irregular hexagon. This need not be a plain area; it could be subdivided into triangles, separated into strips, constructed with the Log Cabin technique or appliquéd with a motif.

4 Introduce colour and texture in an inventive manner, and develop unusual and contrasting tints and tones.

Projects for Three-dimensional Patchwork
You will find many opportunities for using this fascinating form of patchwork. Begin with a cushion, or perhaps a bag or other household item. If you start with a small project there is more incentive to complete it.

Later, having mastered the technique you can expand and adapt the designs to make elegant quilts and wall-hangings. Alternatively, you could reduce the templates to make miniature pieces of work. In the meantime keep your eyes open for design sources. Look at buildings – their structure and their decoration; visit exhibitions; search in the library for more inspiration. There are many avenues to be explored.

Log Cabin
and Log Cabin Houses

Dorothy Stapleton

Dorothy Stapleton trained as a potter at Wimbledon and The Central School of Art, in London. She has taught and exhibited various crafts over the years, but since about 1980 has concentrated on patchwork. She does work to commission, and some of her quilts are now in Norway, the United States, Australia and New Zealand. But she prefers giving her quilts as presents to members of her large family. She usually pieces on the machine but always quilts by hand.

Sources and Approaches

The thing about patchwork that really appeals to me is the thriftiness. I prefer to work with scraps, cut from dresses bought at jumble sales or collected from other people's throw-outs. Sometimes, of course, I am seduced by lovely materials in shops, but not too often. I colour-code my fabrics in stackable boxes to make selection easier when beginning a project.

I began to get hooked on Log Cabin after my first attempts ten years ago; I like the design possibilities of working from such simple strips within a rigid framework. My current obsession with houses started when I was experimenting trying to make pictures with this technique. Perhaps there is a subconscious element in this, for in my other persona I work as a secretary to my husband, a surveyor, and buildings figure prominently in my life.

Log Cabin patchwork seems to have originated in North America during the nineteenth century. There are examples of quilts from the 1880s, including some made out of thin hat ribbons with beautiful effect. It is a technique that can be made from lightweight and other floppy materials, as it is normally made on a backing fabric. The name is derived from the early American settlers' log cabins. According to tradition, the centre square should be red to signify the hearth; the light strips suggest the glow from the fire, and the dark strips the shadows. The basic blocks, constructed in a spiralling fashion, can then be arranged in many ways. In another version, known as Courthouse Steps, the strips are applied to opposite sides alternately. I use both techniques in my work.

Round and Round the Garden
(previous page)

The light sides are all of the same grey-blue fabric and the dark sides various prints ranging from light to dark arranged in concentric circles to form the "Barn Raising" pattern.

99 × 99 in/252 × 252 cm

▼ **Autumn in Oakdene Way**

This portrays the suburbs, hence the three flying ducks in the sky! The bungalows are formed from a house unit without two of the window blocks. I experimented here with using autumn colours for the trees instead of the usual green fabrics and the sky is made up of many different fabrics to resemble clouds.

20 × 42½ in/51 × 108 cm

Miniature Log Cabin ▶

This small quilt is made up of 36 blocks each set around a central red square, all hand sewn. The light and dark fabrics are arranged in the traditional spiral method as described below.

13 × 13 in/33 × 33 cm

Sea Vue Cottage ▽

The house is made from a single unit plus extra roof and window units at the side. The beach and the sea are made up from the same units.

18 × 27 in/46 × 69 cm

Le Manoir ▶

The long drive up to the three-storey house gives this a French feel. The border is heavily quilted with flowers and clouds and smoke in a contrasting thread and a second scrap border added to frame the quilt.

27 × 33 in/69 × 85 cm

The Manor House

I wanted to make a larger, formal-looking house. The manor house has three blocks across and the dark slate roof has a dormer window in the centre section. The central door is assembled to look like a porch or portico. There are garden paths made with slate-effect fabric surrounding lawns. The slight colour grading in the sky has been achieved with tie-dyed and reversed fabrics.

29 × 29 in/74 × 74 cm

Constructing a Log Cabin Block

I use two different methods of construction: the Spiral (here called Method A) and the Courthouse Steps (Method B).

All samples have centre squares of 1½ in/3.8 cm and strips of 1 in/2.5 cm. I cut these as long as the fabric will allow – using a rotary cutter and a large plastic ruler. All strips must be cut on the straight grain of the fabric. All blocks are built up by adding strips to the central square.

Method A (Spiral)

1 Place a light strip face down on the square, edges matching. Machine stitch ¼ in/6 mm from the edge, using the presser foot as a guide. Trim the strip to fit, and press it outwards (see diagram 1a).

1a

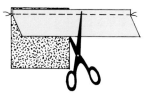

2 Sew the 2nd light strip to the square and the first strip, trim it to fit, and press it outwards as shown (see diagram 1b).

1b

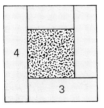

3 Continuing in a clockwise direction, sew strip 3 (dark) to the square and strip 2.

4 Sew strip 4 (dark) to strip 3, the square and strip 1 to complete the first round (see diagram 1c).

1c

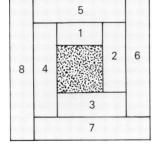

5 Continue adding light and dark until the block is the required size (see diagram 1d). Note that the last strip of every round extends over the whole side of that round. The strips can be graded from light to dark within each side, but take care not to use the same fabric as a dark-light and as a light-dark. It helps to keep the strips in separate bags.

1d

Method B (Courthouse Steps)

The effect of steps is created by piecing the lights and darks in a different order, placing dark opposite dark, light opposite light and working across the square instead of around it. Normally the longer strips of each round are placed horizontally (you can see this effect by turning the page 90°); but I have shown the block with the longer strips vertical, as this is how they are placed in the house pictures.

1 Join a light strip to the square as for Method A (see diagram 1a).

2 Sew a strip 2 (light) to the opposite side of the square (see diagram 2a).

2a

3 Sew a strip 3 (dark) on the right-hand side, across the square and strips 1 and 2.

4 Sew a strip 4 (dark) opposite strip 3 (see diagram 2b).

2b

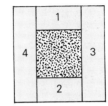

5 Continue adding strips on opposite sides until the block is the required size (see diagram 2c).

2c

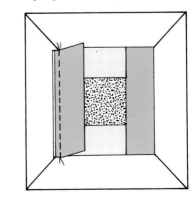

Special Methods

If you are sewing by hand, Log Cabin is best constructed on a backing fabric, which can have diagonal lines drawn onto it so as to make it easier to get the strips straight (see diagram 3). I find that checked shirting is useful for this purpose, as it provides horizontal guide-

3

lines also; but make sure that the squares are accurate. This method is especially recommended for flimsy fabric such as lawn, which can become distorted with the single-thickness method.

Blocks can also be assembled in the quilt-as-you-go method, with a square of thin wadding over the backing and the strips sewn to both layers (see diagram 4).

4

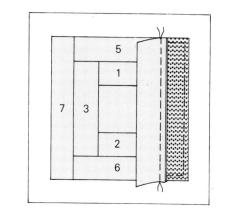

If you are making several identical Log Cabin blocks, a good method to use on the first round is continuous line sewing.

Sew all the squares required to the first strip, leaving a gap between each square. Trim the strips to size (see diagram 5), and press. Join the following strips in the same way (see diagram 6). This method is especially useful when the unit is very small. I place the units in a small basket when assembling many at a time; otherwise they tend to get lost.

5   6

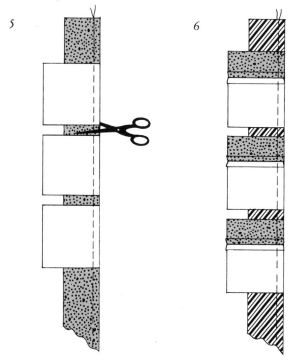

Materials

Scraps of closely woven fabric to represent bricks, stonework, roof, chimney, sky, foliage, tree trunks, grass, paving, flower beds, door and curtains

For border, dark-coloured fabric, any width; ⅜ yard/ 40 cm (this will make a simple border; you can make a more complex one, as shown in the photograph, from additional strips of fabric)

For backing, any suitable fabric: piece approximately 29 × 23 in/74 × 59 cm

Lightweight (2-ounce) wadding: piece same size as backing fabric

Drawing and sewing materials (see page 10)

A Log Cabin House

The following instructions describe how to make a house similar to "Le Manoir" shown on page 107. Both Method A and Method B are used to create the different elements, such as houses, trees and paths.

The completed picture measures approximately 29 × 23 in/74 × 59 cm, excluding the borders.

Choosing the Fabrics

It is great fun looking for fabrics to represent roofs, walls, flowers, trees, sky, and other parts of the picture. The rule to remember is not to muddle the "currency": if a certain fabric is representing a brick wall, the same fabric cannot represent a flower bed, even if it is a floral print, for this would confuse the eye. I cut up lots of 1 in/2.5 cm strips with the rotary cutter, then bag them up into the different elements, labelling them "sky", "walls", and so on.

Cutting the Pieces

I use 1½ in/3.8 cm squares for the centres; all strips are 1 in/2.5 cm wide, which when sewn gives a finished width of ½ in/1.2 cm.

Windows

1   Cut the centre squares of either black or yellow fabric, or both, depending on whether you wish to show lights off or on. You can create a leaded light effect window with checked material. Curtains or blinds (see diagram 7) can be cut from any suitable scraps, sewn onto the window along their inner edges, then turned back, pressed and trimmed as required. Small-patterned lace makes pretty curtains.

7

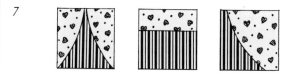

2 Using Method B, add strips 1 and 2 for the window surrounds, cut from a stone-effect fabric; this must contrast with the fabric that you will use for bricks (see diagram 8).

A floral fabric could be used for strip 2 to suggest a window box.

8

3 Add strips 3 and 4 to complete the round, using either brick fabric or a suitably coloured plain fabric to represent shutters (see diagram 9).

9

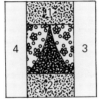

4 On the second round, add a strip (5) of window frame material to suggest a pediment. Strip 6 is cut out of brick fabric (see diagram 10). Strips 7 and 8 should both be brick for the upper blocks, but use a plain-coloured strip at the adjacent edges of the ground-floor blocks for the front door (see diagram 11).

10

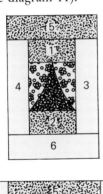

11

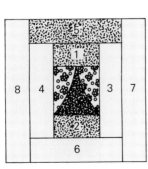

5 Make and join 6 blocks for the house shown, taking ¼ in/6 mm seam allowance.

Roofs

These are assembled using Method A.

1 Cut 2 triangles of sky material and 2 of roof fabric, and join them to make a 1½ in/3.8 cm square (as shown in the photograph below).

2 Join a strip (1) of sky to one sky edge of the square. (The choice of edge depends on which way the roof is to slant.) Join a brick strip of fabric (2) to the adjacent edge of sky to form a chimney (see photograph).

3 Add roof strips (3 and 4) to complete the first round (see photograph).

4 On the next round add 2 sky strips (5 and 6) to the sky and chimney, then add 2 roof strips (7 and 8). This completes the roof block (see photograph).

5 Make 2 blocks in this way, each a mirror image of the other (the chimney could be omitted on one). Join them down the centre, making sure the sky is on the outer edge. Press the work and sew it to the house.

Trees

These are assembled by Method A. Each tree contains 4 blocks.

1 Cut 4 green centre squares.

2 Join strips as follows (working clockwise on all blocks): 1 sky, 2 sky, 3 foliage, 4 foliage, 5 sky, 6 sky, 7 foliage, 8 foliage (as shown in the photograph below).

3 Assemble the 4 blocks with the sky on the outer edges.

4 For the house shown, make another identical block, and 2 blocks using grass instead of sky.

Tree Trunk

1 Cut 2 centre squares of floral fabric.

2 Add strips of various floral fabrics, using Method B, until the last strip, which is the trunk, in brown (see photograph).

3 Sew the trunk block to the tree. The completed unit contains 6 blocks.

Trees do not have to be green; you could use glowing autumn colours instead. Likewise, sky could be blue, white, grey, pink or a mixture, including cloud effects.

Paving

This can be made out of random shades of grey using Method B.

Walls

Two different walls are used for the house shown. Both use Method B, but here the longer strips are placed horizontally as in the traditional Courthouse Steps pattern. Follow the arrangements shown, or devise different ones. You will need 4 wall units for the back wall and 6 for the front one (see diagram 12).

12

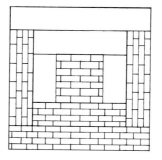

Other House and Garden Blocks

Garden paths are made the same as tree trunks, using Method B, but the last strip, instead of being brown, is a brick fabric (see diagram 13).

13

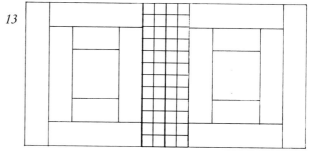

A topiary hedge effect can be made with central square and rows 2 and 6 in green, the rest in a floral print (see diagram 14).

14

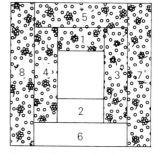

A formal garden (either method) could have the central square either grass or flowers, with rows 1 to 4 brick or slate and rows 5 to 8 flowers or grass.

A pond could be made by cutting the square and rows 1 to 4 in water fabric, the rest in grass.

Assembling the Picture

1 Join the completed blocks as shown in diagram 15, taking ¼ in/6 mm seam allowance. Press the seams open.

2 For the simple border, cut 2 strips each measuring 30 × 3½ in/76 × 8.5 cm and 2 strips each measuring 19 × 3½ in/48 × 8.5 cm. Sew the shorter strips to the top and bottom edges of the picture, then sew the long strips to the sides, including the top and bottom borders. (A seam allowance of ½ in/1 cm is included – ¼ in/6 mm on the picture itself.)

If you like, you can create a more elaborate border, as shown in the photograph. A strip border makes a nice touch. This consists of left-over strips from the patchwork, joined in a long strip and cut to the required lengths.

3 Place the top, wadding and backing layers together, and tack from side to side.

If you wish to add some quilting (the many seams make this rather difficult), you might use it to suggest smoke from chimneys, clouds, cobbles or birds. I usually let the quilting "escape" into the border, where it is easier to work, as there are no seams.

The picture could also be tied (see page 93), which holds the layers together and is a quicker method of finishing.

4 Turn under the edges of the border, enclosing wadding and backing, and hem them neatly in place.

The units can, of course, be used in different ways to make a quite different house or even a whole town.

15

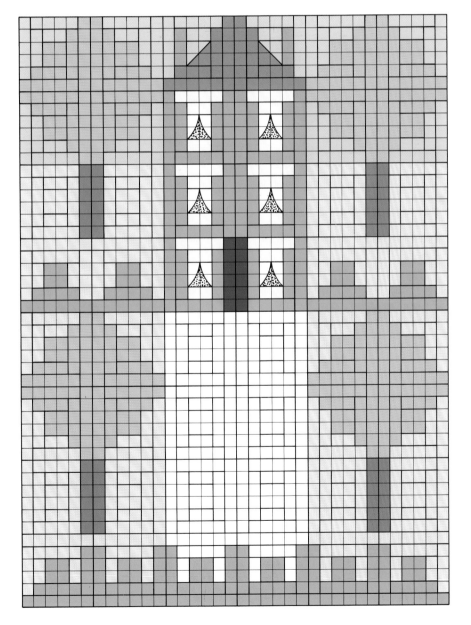

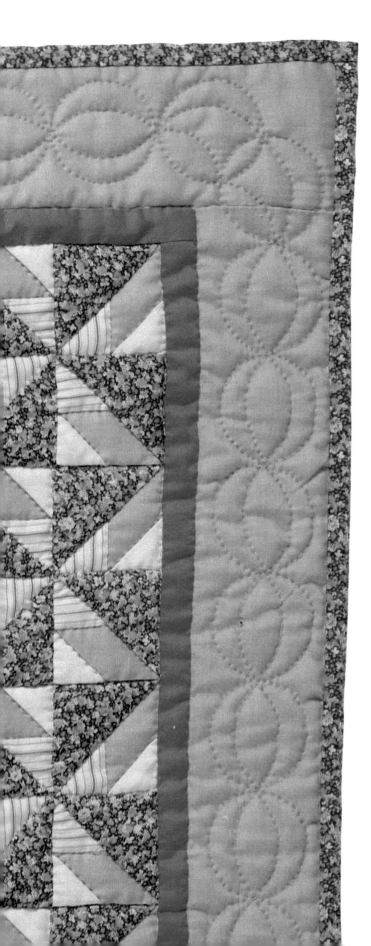

Quilts for Dolls
and Dolls' Houses

Edyth Henry

Having discovered quiltmaking early in 1979 and immediately become hooked, Edyth Henry, like all converts, wanted to share her enthusiasm with everybody. In 1983 she started teaching beginners to make sampler quilts. She then specialized in Hawaiian quilts and, later, dolls' quilts, giving workshops and talks to raise funds for the British Quilters' Guild, of which she is a founder member. Being now past retirement age, she no longer teaches regular classes but hopes to continue workshops and talks indefinitely.

Sources and Approaches

Being a craftworker rather than an artist, I am fascinated by techniques and have explored most of them at one time or another. Perhaps the most interesting discovery was that in quiltmaking there are more ways than one of doing practically everything. It is not a case of one way being right and another wrong, but rather that different methods suit different people. And since there are so many alternatives already, it is open to anyone to experiment further.

My interest in dolls' quilts began in January 1987, with an article in an American publication, *The Quilter's Newsletter Magazine*, about Tina Gravatt, who had made a collection of quilts to a scale of approximately 1:4, to depict the rich history of quilts from 1750 to the present. And there they were – perfect replicas of the real thing.

This surely was a practical proposition and provided an answer to a problem of mine, which was that I clearly would never have enough time to make all the full-size quilts that I wanted to make, nor would I have enough space, since every bed in my family already had at least two quilts. Doll-size quilts could well be the solution.

My first attempt was a near-disaster. As usual, I had used cotton fabrics and lightweight, 2-ounce wadding. The result was stiff and un-yielding, and the quilting stitches looked enormous. What was meant to be a doll's quilt had turned out to be a passable wall-hanging. No self-respecting doll would have had it on her bed.

I still work with cotton fabrics, but am careful to choose lightweight ones, such as Liberty lawn. Some polyester cotton blends are also suitable. A mixture of fabrics seems to work quite well – always provided that they are light in weight. And I have found a variety of solutions (discussed below) to the wadding problem.

Many dolls' quilts look wrong to me because the scale of the patch-

Easebourne Challenge
(previous page)

One of my first successful dolls' quilts, this was made for an annual exhibition organized by Angela Brocklebank at Easebourne Priory, near Midhurst, Sussex. The challenge was to design some patchwork based on three shapes: two right-angled triangles (one half the size of the other) and a parallelogram. The resulting block may well be an existing traditional pattern, though I designed it independently. The fabrics, apart from the plain blue, are Liberty prints. An empty thread reel served as a template for the simple chain design used for the border quilting.

17 × 20 in/43 × 51 cm

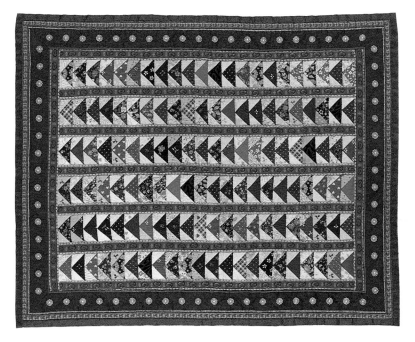

◀ **Flying Geese**

This is far and away my favourite among my dolls' quilts. I have always liked the pattern, and on this occasion all the elements seemed to fall into place naturally. I love the glowing colours of the triangles – cut from dozens of fabric samples obtained from quilting shops. The little circles of the striped border fabric suggested the design for the quilting on this part of the quilt. I was very pleased when this quilt won the Visitors' Choice ribbon at an exhibition in Wimborne, Dorset, in 1988.

11½ × 14½ in/29 × 37 cm

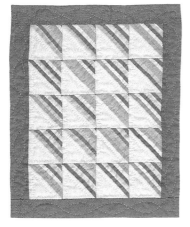

▲ **Rail Fence and Roman Stripe**

The same striped fabric was used in both of these little quilts. For "Rail Fence" (top) I cut squares all from the same section of the fabric.

For "Roman Stripe" I placed the triangular template on different parts of the striped fabric, so that nearly all the triangles are different.

Rail Fence, 6 × 7 in/15 × 18 cm; Roman Stripe, 8 × 9 in/20 × 23 cm

Grandmother's Flower Garden ▶

*A total of 770 hexagons were used for this quilt, pieced in the traditional English way.
The quilt contains no wadding; it is flat-quilted on the flower centres and along the "paths" only.*

17 × 20 in/43 × 51 cm

work is too large in proportion to the size of the quilt. I wanted mine to look right. At first I restricted my efforts to a scale of either 1:4 or 1:12, the latter being the accepted scale for miniatures; but my granddaughter cured me of such inflexibility; "Dolls", she said firmly, "come in all sizes". So, now, do my quilts.

Once I had made two or three successful quilts with American blocks, it occurred to me that other techniques were worth exploring and possibly developing into a workshop. Some of these techniques, such as hexagons, Log Cabin and Cathedral Window, would obviously be very time-consuming, but would appeal to those who enjoy painstaking handwork. There would also need to be quicker techniques for those quilters who are always looking for something that can be finished "yesterday".

For me, quiltmaking is an art of illusion. A quilt artist brings movement and life to the work by the manipulation of colour and tone. Quilts in which every seam is straight can appear to be a mass of interlocking circles, and others can look three-dimensional. Dyes and fabric paints can be employed to enhance the illusion, as can stencils, embroidery and other embellishments. Similar illusions can be used in dolls' quilts to make them appear genuine.

Stripes are the most obvious creators of illusion. Anything that could be done wih strips of fabric sewn together and re-cut could surely be suggested by striped fabric, provided suitable stripes could be found. This was not easy. Everybody in the street seemed to be wearing the fabrics I was looking for; but I could not find them in the shops. So I tried the opposite approach, exploring fabrics that *were* available and drawing inspiration from them. This was much more rewarding, and the ideas began to flow. I now found myself looking at all fabrics with new eyes, and my collection of dolls' quilts began to grow.

◀ **Barn Raising**

*The 64 blocks used for this
traditional Log Cabin design
measure 1¾ in/4.5 cm square. The
strips were sewn to squares of
gingham, working from the
wrong side and using the lines of
checks as a guide. Again, I used
fabric samples from quilting shops
for the patchwork – 832 pieces.
This quilt won Second Prize in the
Dolls' Quilts section of Quilts
U.K. 1989.*

14½ × 14½ in/37 × 37 cm

Making Dolls' Quilts

Experience of stitching patchwork to a normal scale is
helpful when working the small quilts in this workshop.
When reducing the scale of quilts to doll-size, it is often
necessary to adapt techniques, or even invent new ones.
This workshop includes some of the methods I have
devised, which I hope you will find useful. But why not
do some experimenting yourself? You could find a
method that suits you better. If the desired result is
achieved, the method is irrelevant.

The workshop also includes instructions for making
four quilts: a medallion quilt using triangles cut from
striped fabric; two quilts using shadow quilting; and
one quilt using a variation of the Cathedral Window
technique.

It is important to remember that the objective – whatever the technique used – is to make a small replica of a
real quilt, in which everything is to scale. To do
this, accuracy is vital, and stitches need to be as small as
possible. Slight inaccuracies in piecing that could be
accommodated in, say, a 12 in/30 cm block would, in a
3 in/8 cm block, be disastrous.

Basic Materials and Methods

Needles The finer the needle, the finer (potentially) the
stitch; so try a smaller size needle than you normally
use. A 10–12 betweens is ideal, but an equally fine sharp
is a good substitute if you prefer.

Thread Fine sewing thread should be used for quilting,
rather than the heavier quilting thread. Thread that
matches the fabric makes unobtrusive stitches which
sink into the line of shadow.

Wadding, if used needs to be as thin as possible. Sometimes a quilt shop will have a bolt of 2-ounce wadding
that appears to be very thin. Everybody is complaining
about it – except those making dolls' quilts! An alternative is to strip the bonded outside layers from thicker
wadding. The soft middle can be teased out to provide a
really thin layer. In the United States you can buy very
thin, flat wadding made of 80 percent cotton and 20
percent polyester which is well suited to the purpose.
Silk wadding (available by mail order) is lovely to use. It
is expensive, but a little goes a long way when making
dolls' quilts. For very small quilts, such as those for
dolls' houses, soft, fleecy domette works well.

Templates may be made from graph paper and card (for squares, right-angled triangles, rectangles) or from template plastic; the kind marked with a grid is especially useful.

Seam allowances of ¼ in/6 mm are easier to handle than very narrow ones; they can be trimmed after stitching. Running stitch is used, except for English patchwork, which is oversewn in the usual way.

Quilting should be kept simple. Quilt in the ditch on the patchwork, and use simple chain patterns on the borders. In this way the results appear much less clumsy than if complex quilting designs were attempted.

English Patchwork

The method of constructing miniature English patchwork is essentially the same as for the full-size version (see page 101). It is possible to buy quite small metal templates, but I have found it simpler and more accurate to bypass these and to cut the papers from isometric paper (or squared paper if appropriate).

To cut the papers for 1 cm (⅜ in) hexagons, first cut a strip of isometric paper 4 rows deep. Then mark and cut diamonds, 4 rows wide (see diagram 1a). Trim off the corners (diagram 1b) to get the hexagons.

1a

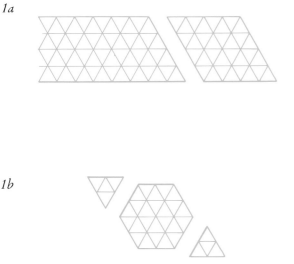

1b

Cut out the fabric shapes, adding seam allowance as usual. To hold the fabric shapes in place while tacking the edges, do not pin (which would distort the papers and get in the way), but sew a little cross stitch in the centre – as in sewing on a button. Then tack the edges over the papers and continue as usual.

Log Cabin

Bearing in mind the technique developed by Rita Humphry for her Whirlies, I found that by using gingham for a base fabric and sewing the logs from the back, small-scale Log Cabin blocks could be made with great accuracy and without templates. The main difference is that I sew by hand.

Look for a lightweight polyester cotton gingham or checked fabric. I have used a gingham with ¼ in/6 mm checks for the quilt photographed on page 118.

Striped Designs

Stripes are wonderful for creating illusions. One of the main problems in dolls' quilts is bulk, especially in seams. It is often possible to eliminate nearly half the seams in a block by placing templates across stripes. Thus blocks such as Shoo-fly or Sherman's March (see diagram 2) can be made from only nine pieces, instead of the 13 or 17 normally required. Vertical and horizontal "joins" can be created as in diagram 3a; diagonal ones as in diagram 3b.

2

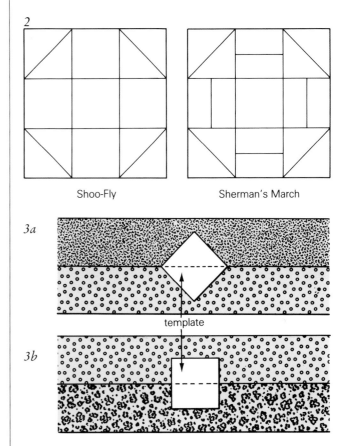

Shoo-Fly   Sherman's March

3a

template

3b

The basic procedure in these striped designs is first to identify the stripes needed and mark the fabric, then to add seam allowances and cut out the pieces. By quilting along the stripes, as well as the actual seams, one strengthens the illusion.

Medallion Quilt from Stripes

A Medallion quilt consists of a framed central design with a number of borders which have a proportional relationship to this centre section. Only two templates are needed for this quilt: both right-angled triangles. These are shown in the plan for the quilt (see diagram 4). The longest side of Template 1 should measure half the width of the finished quilt without borders. Template 2 is half the size of Template 1. The quilt shown measures 17 × 21 in/43 × 53 cm.

4

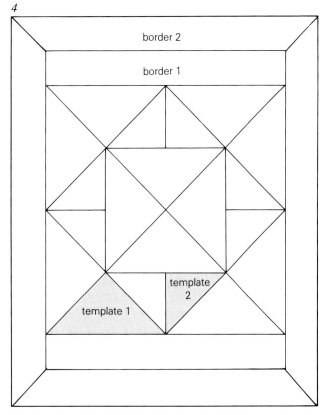

Materials
For patchwork, striped fabric, any width: ⅝ yard/60 cm
For backing, piece of fabric approximately 18 × 22 in/46 × 56 cm
Thin wadding, piece same size as backing
2 mirror tiles or handbag mirrors
Drawing and sewing materials (see page 10)

1 Draw the design to the required size on graph paper. The width of the borders can be adjusted as desired. Square quilts for dolls tend to look like cushion covers or pot holders, so I always add an extra border at top and bottom before the final border.

2 Make window templates for the 2 triangles by cutting the template shapes out of squares of cardboard.

Try them in various positions on the stripes, using mirrors to see how 2 or 4 will look when joined.

3 Mark and cut out 12 large triangles and 8 small ones. Remember to add seam allowances.

4 Join the 4 large triangles of the centre square, then join the smaller triangles together in pairs and add to the centre square. Finally join the remaining large triangles in pairs and add to complete the main section of the quilt.

5 Cut 2 strips for Border 1 to fit the top and bottom of the patchwork (remembering to add seam allowance) and an appropriate width for the fabric you are using. Sew these in place.

6 Cut 4 strips for Border 2, cutting each the length of a side, plus twice the chosen width of the border, plus seam allowances. Sew each to the patchwork, allowing the excess to overlap at the corners, then mitre the corners as shown on page 93.

7 Cut the wadding and backing slightly larger than the quilt top. Assemble the three layers and tack them together (see page 16). Work the quilting as desired.

8 Trim the wadding. Turn under the raw edges of both backing and border, and quilt them together.

Shadow Quilting

More illusions can be produced with shadow quilting, which simulates patchwork surprisingly effectively. Here are two traditional designs to try.

Drunkard's Path

The "Drunkard's Path" template is simply a circle used in conjunction with an underlying grid. "A Thousand Pyramids" is composed of equilateral triangles, divided into light and dark tones. Note that the same colour can serve as light in a dark context or dark in a light one, within the same quilt. (See the comments on tonal values on page 154.)

Materials

A piece of calico slightly larger than the finished quilt (the one shown measures 10 × 12 in/25 × 30 cm)

For "patchwork", backing and binding, a piece of contrasting fabric one-and-a-half times the size of the calico

A piece of white organza the same size as the calico

Fabric glue

Drawing and sewing materials (see page 10)

1 On a piece of paper draw a 1 in/2.5 cm square grid the size of the finished patchwork. The grid must contain a multiple of 4 squares; here the number is 80. Go over the lines with a broad felt-tip pen so that they can be seen through calico. Pin the grid to a cork board, or tape it to another smooth surface.

2 Trace the circle (diagram 5) and make a template.

5

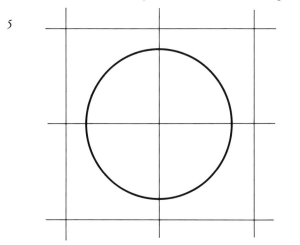

3 Cut a piece of contrasting fabric slightly more than half the size of the grid. Pin it over the grid and transfer the grid lines onto the fabric with a ruler and pencil, or other marker, to make a grid containing half the total number of squares – in this case, 40.

4 Centre the circular template on each group of 4 squares and draw around it.

5 Cut along all the lines with sharp scissors; each 4-square group will thus yield 4 quarter circles and 4 curved corners. (A pair of nail scissors is ideal for cutting the curves.) Note that no seam allowances are needed with this technique.

6 Pin the piece of calico over the grid. Position the cut pieces as shown in diagram 6 (and also in the photograph), sticking them down with a dab of glue.

6

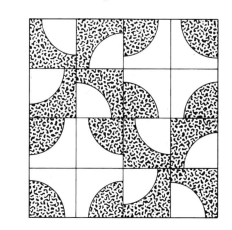

7 Carefully remove the work from the board. Cover it with a layer of organza or chiffon, and assemble the quilt sandwich in the usual way (see page 16) with wadding and backing. Tack thoroughly.

8 Quilt along the grid lines and around the curves. In this way all the raw edges are surrounded with quilting and cannot shift or unravel.

9 Bind the edges (see page 17) with the patchwork fabric or another suitable fabric.

Thousand Pyramids

This quilt is made in basically the same way as "Drunk-ard's Path" but on a triangular grid and using organza instead of calico as the base fabric. This helps to reduce bulk. Do be careful, though, that the organza does not stick to the grid. Pass a ruler between the two layers from time to time when gluing the triangles.

Materials

2 pieces of white organza, the size of the finished quilt (the one shown measures 10 × 12 in/25 × 30 cm)

For "patchwork" a variety of fabric scraps in light and dark tones

For backing, a piece of fabric slightly larger than the quilt

Fabric glue

Drawing and sewing materials (see page 10)

1   To make the complete grid, trace the small section given (diagram 7) in the centre of a piece of paper, then extend the lines to make a grid of the required size. The quilt shown has 11 triangles across and 17 down.

2   Darken the lines with a felt-tip pen. Pin chosen scraps, one at a time, onto the grid and transfer the grid lines onto the fabric with a ruler and pencil or other marker.

3   Cut triangles apart with sharp scissors.

4   Place a piece of organza over the grid and pin or tape it firmly in place.

5   Arrange and re-arrange the triangles on the organza until you are satisfied with the result. Glue them lightly in place.

6   Lay the other piece of organza on top and complete the quilt as for "Drunkard's Path".

Remember that with shadow quilting all the raw edges of the individual pieces must be completely enclosed by quilting lines.

Cathedral Window

The scale of Cathedral Window patchwork may be re-duced by a slight adaptation of a well-known method. Instead of stitching the first seams, then turning through, the stitching is done from the right side.

The doll's quilt shown measures about 12 × 14 in/30 × 36 cm and contains 72 windows.

7

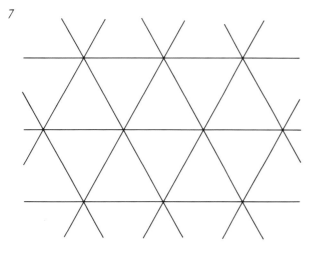

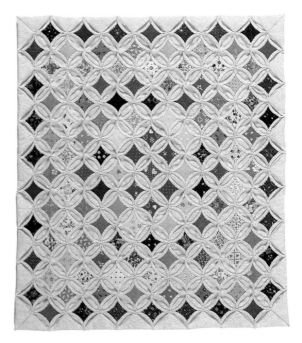

Materials

For blocks, plain-coloured cotton fabric, 36 in/90 cm
   wide: ⅞ yard/80 cm
For windows, assorted contrasting fabrics
Drawing and sewing materials (see page 10)

1 Cut a template 3 in/7.5 cm square from thin cardboard. Cut fabric 3½ in/9 cm square, and iron the seam
allowances over the template (see diagram 8a). Remove
the template and press again.

8a

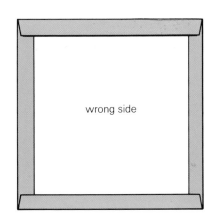

2 Fold the square in half, raw edges inside, and slipstitch up both sides (see diagram 8b).

8b

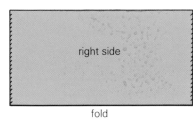

3 Fold the sides inwards so that the seams meet in the
middle, and slipstitch right across (see diagram 8c).

8c

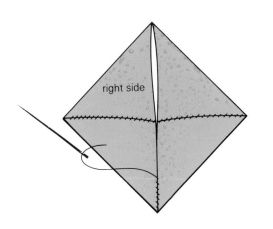

4 Fold two corners to the middle, and stitch firmly
two or three times through all layers (see diagram 8d).
Fold the other two corners to the middle, and stitch
them together through the bar just worked (see diagram
8e). The resulting unit is 1½ in/3.8 cm square, one-
quarter the size of the original template.

8d   *8e*

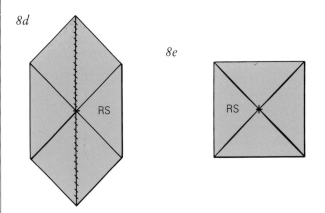

5 Make another unit in the same way. Place the two
back to back and oversew them neatly together (see diagram 8f).

8f

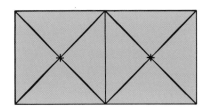

6 Insert a contrasting square and stitch in the usual
way (see diagram 8g and page 88). If pins get in the way,
tack the contrasting square in position with a cross
stitch, which can be removed later.

8g

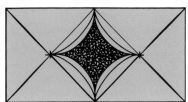

7 Make up and join the required number of units for
the quilt.

To reduce the size still further, try using a smaller template. With a template smaller than 2 in/5 cm square, the
window inserts get very difficult to handle. My one and
only real miniature quilt is a Cathedral Window cot quilt
measuring 4 × 5 in/10 × 13 cm. For this I used a template 1¼ in/3.2 cm square. It took a very long time to
make!

Curves

Annette Claxton

Annette Claxton taught in adult education for ten years, starting with dressmaking and quilted clothes. Gradually, patchwork and quilting "took over" as she increasingly discovered – and shared with her students – the creative possibilities in quiltmaking.

She now teaches workshops and gives talks aimed at helping students gain the confidence to design and make original patchwork. Her particular interest is modern quilts, especially wallhangings using curved seams. She uses traditional methods, piecing by machine and quilting by hand, often working in silk.

Sources and Approaches

Like many quilters, I was first introduced to quilts through American books on patchwork, learning to use the nine patch, and the repeated block. My first quilt was a scrap, unquilted bedcover, composed of 3 in/7.5 cm squares, made from material begged from friends. Fired by the stimulation of working with colour and pattern, I made another, this time in 4 in/10 cm velvet squares. I knew nothing about textiles, so as the squares gradually pulled apart due to the incompatibility of cotton and rayon velvet, it became obvious that something was wrong with my technique. A four-year part-time course in fashion taught me to sew properly, and opened up undreamt-of possibilities.

I am currently working with curves, triangles and diagonals. These geometric shapes have been inspired by Art Deco designs, by abstract paintings by such artists as Paul Klee, Robert and Sonya Delaunay, and Frank Stella, and by post-modern architecture. I find the circle a very satisfying shape and the dynamics of diagonals exciting; triangles suggest movement, rather like arrows.

Most of my quilts are for walls, although I do make some bed quilts and clothing from time to time. I love the effect of silk as the light catches and reflects the texture, and I have a store of lengths in colours that I know will be used. These always have to be supplemented as a quilt takes shape, but at least the basics are there.

Working with silk is not always easy; I use Indian dupion, which frays very quickly, so the seam allowance has to be slightly wider than the usual ¼ in/6 mm and it must be pressed with a dry iron. It continues to fray once pieced, so requires a light touch and quick work to get it finished and tacked to the wadding and backing.

Likewise I have a store of cotton fabrics. Pure cotton is wonderful to work with, obedient, good tempered; it presses flat, giving a crisp, clean seam. I rarely use florals but have a small collection of what I call "razzle dazzle". These cotton prints were acquired during a visit to Australia, where bright patterns are worn by people of all ages, and complement the light and the lifestyle. They look quite different in Britain's cold northern light, but they are in my quilt "Down Under".

Before I start to work on a quilt, I spend some time looking through books, postcards and photographs. The profusion of images is very stimulating, but eventually decisions must be made, visions transferred to paper. I prepare several pages of 4 in/10 cm squares on layout paper. In these squares I draw my first designs, adding colour to the promising ones, leaving many unfinished as an idea goes cold, working fairly quickly. I select two or three of the best designs and enlarge them 6–8 in/15–20 cm. These are left to "rest" until somehow one design seems right. The next step is to draw the design full size on dressmaker's squared pattern paper. In the meantime, I have scattered in my workroom the fabrics that are under consideration, and I occasionally sneak glances around the door in order to see them with fresh eyes and gauge their effect more objectively.

I then pin the design to the workroom wall and pin the fabrics, folded roughly to shape, over it, so that I can judge the effect. I num-

Down Under
(previous page)

After a visit to Australia in 1989, I felt inspired to make a quilt of my impressions of the trip. Although we visited only the East Coast, we saw a great variety of landscape, which is reflected in the quilt. In Queensland we saw rainforests: dark, tall trees – a quite different green from the soft greens of England. Palms on the coast, the huge sky and sea, together with surf breaking against the shore, were another influence. The colours of the birds and of the fish in the Great Barrier Reef were as bright as the flowers on trees and in gardens. The tall buildings of Sydney and houses with cool verandahs are juxtaposed with images of Bondi Beach. Rita Humphry's Whirly technique was used, large scale, to piece the sky. The hanging is machine-pieced and hand-quilted, both "in-the-ditch" and in the tiled roof of the Sydney Opera House.

60 × 60 in/152 × 152 cm

Max: Sleeping for England ▶

This quilt is for our first grandchild. The room has been papered in yellow and green stripes, with balloons and a train frieze. I wanted it to be a stimulating quilt, echoing the theme of the room. The little 1 in/ 2.5 cm squares look like flags. The curved flying geese and leopard spots and the diagonals make it a quilt full of movement. It is machine quilted.

28 × 40 in/71 × 102 cm

ber the pieces on both the large and small drawings, adding grain lines and balance marks to assist in the assembly. Then I cut up the full-size design to use as templates. These are placed on the wrong side of the fabric and drawn around in soft pencil, then cut out. As the pieces are joined they are pinned to the wall. I piece the work by machine, working on small areas at a time and assembling the whole only when I am satisfied that the colours and sewing are right. This means that units can be discarded if they are not working and another combination inserted. Again, I used the "peep round the door" method to catch sight of the quilt unexpectedly; I also photograph it, for often the emphasis seems to change on film. At last, the piecing is finished and the time comes to tack the wadding and backing together. I like tacking, with its rhythmic, calming effect. I hand quilt on a floor frame. This has the advantage of keeping the work flat and clean. An hour's quilting can be snatched without having to clear a space or sweep the floor first.

Although I urge students to use a thimble, I am unable to work with one, so I cut a small circle of leather and tape it over my top finger, but use a thimble on my underneath hand. When the quilt is finished, I like to hang the quilt up and look at it for a while. I feel quite drained and flat, having worked on the quilt for perhaps three months.

▼ **Windows 1**

The possibilities of using windows as a design source led to a series of window quilts. My only brief for this commission was "bright" and "primary". It is machine-pieced and quilted by hand.

28 × 52 in/71 × 132 cm

Cold Light of Day

This cot quilt was made for a design-conscious couple who were heavily into chrome and black. The title evokes all those early morning feedings. It is machine-pieced and hand-quilted, "in-the-ditch". I wanted it to appear stark and uncluttered.

28 × 40 in/71 × 102 cm

Curves 1

This was my first excursion into curved patchwork. It is machine-pieced and machine-quilted. The quilting is very formal, as I was then trying out the possibilities of using the machine to speed up my output.

28 × 40 in/71 × 102 cm

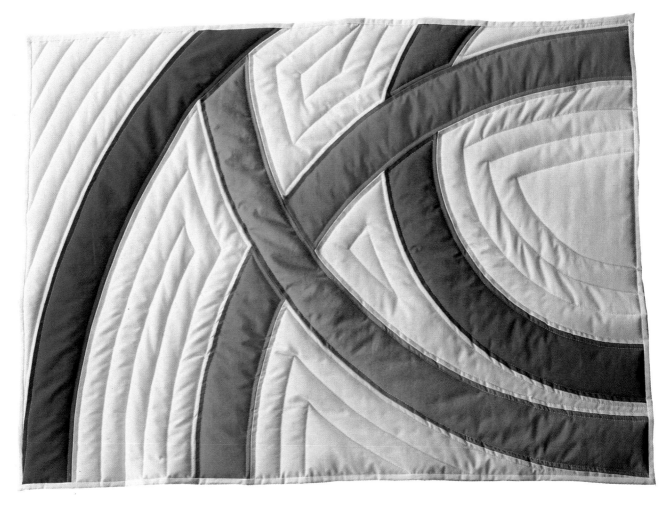

"Breezy" Quilt

"Breezy" is a group quilt, designed and organized by me and made by the Beckenham (Kent) Quilters. After working out the design and making templates, I cut out the fabric, and sixteen people made up the blocks. These were then assembled by other quilters. Still others added the borders, then a tacking party put the top, wadding and back together. The quilt was put onto my floor standing frame, and small bands of quilters came and worked together. Finally we hand-finished the edges and added our label.

The quilt consists of one basic block made up in two closely related colourways: one light, one darker. Bright pink wavy lines join the blocks, and the light and dark blue lines touch and appear to twist. The sixteen complete blocks in the centre are surrounded by twenty partial blocks, which help to create the "open-ended" quality of the design. A bright pink binding contains the movement in the design, which was inspired by a photograph of some crazy paving in a magazine. The finished quilt measures 72 in/183 cm square.

Our quilt has a fairly complex border, consisting of a shocking pink band and a grey band, into which the bright pink wavy lines extend. However, you could simplify the design and the construction by making the quilt entirely of whole blocks and simply binding the edge. The fabric quantities given are ample for either arrangement.

The partial blocks are cut down from whole blocks and measure 7 in/17.9 cm in width – slightly more than half the width of the complete 12 in/30.5 cm block. For our quilt we prepared special templates for these blocks, but this is a very complex procedure. The same effect can be achieved much more simply by making 36 complete blocks and trimming the outer ones to size. This entails some wastage of fabric and time, however; and you may prefer an even simpler option: to make only 10 outer blocks (5 light and 5 dark) and cutting them in half. The resulting partial blocks will measure only 5¾ in/14.5 cm wide (finished), and the quilt will be slightly smaller. Also, the spacious effect of the design will be very slightly diminished.

Materials

For patchwork, lightweight cotton fabrics, 45 in/115 cm wide, in the 2 related colourways (here shades of blue, mauve and pink), as follows:

Template 1   20 in/50 cm each of lighter and darker tones

Template 2   20 in/50 cm each of lighter and darker tones

Template 3   1¼ yards/1 metre each of lighter and darker tones

Template 4   28 in/70 cm each of lighter and darker tones

Template 5   1 yard/90 cm each of lighter and darker tones

Template 6   1⅓ yards/1.25 metres of one colour (here bright pink is used)

Template 7   20 in/50 cm each of lighter and darker tones

Template 8/9   10 in/25 cm of one colour (here black is used)

1

= balance marks

→ grain lines

each square = 3 in/7.5 cm

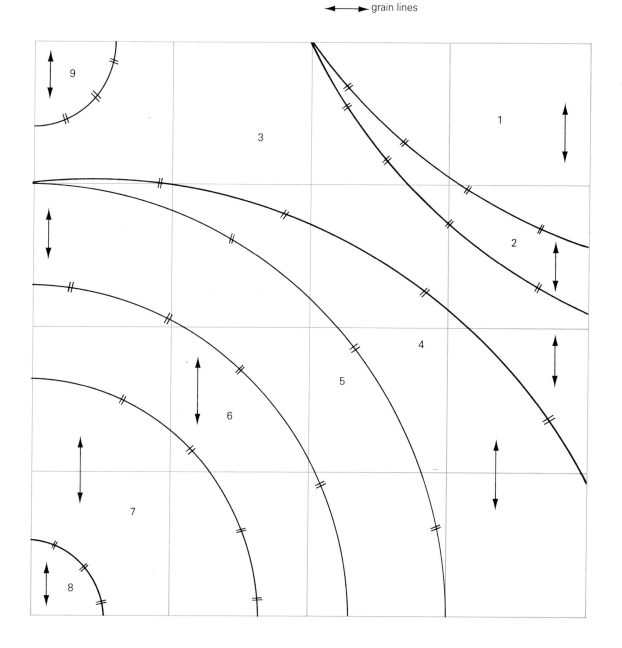

For inner border, 45 in/115 cm-wide fabric (here shocking pink): 1 yard/90 cm

For outer border, 45 in/115 cm-wide fabric (here light grey): 7/8 yard/80 cm

For backing and binding, 45 in/115 cm-wide fabric (here purple): 4½ yards/4 metres

Lightweight (2-ounce) wadding: enough to make (joined if necessary) a piece 73 in/185 cm square

Drawing and sewing materials (see page 10), including dressmaker's carbon and wheel

Making the Patchwork

1 Enlarge the block (see diagram 1) to measure 12 in/ 30.5 cm square (see page 42) on fairly thick paper. *This diagram is shown in reverse from the finished quilt, as you will be marking the piece on the back of the fabric.* (Note also that when joined the light and dark blocks are turned in opposite directions.)

It does not matter if you do not get all the pieces in exactly the same places, so long as the bright pink lines fall in the centre of the two sides and the point of the narrow blue curve is in the top/bottom centre. Check also that the two black quarter circles are the same size.

2 Number all the pieces as in the diagram. Now draw in grain lines and the balance marks, or notches, on the curves. These are *essential* to enable you to piece the block without stretching your fabric.

3 Make a separate accurate tracing of the full-size block. Cut up the drawing – but not the tracing – to use as templates.

4 Now comes the part I particularly enjoy: choosing the fabric colours. Busy prints do not work so well with curved-shape designs, but you can see that the bright pink fabric has a rather strong pattern. One-colour prints and plains are probably best, but stripes can be great fun, so you can experiment.

Prepare the fabrics you have selected as instructed on page 11.

5 Place each template on the wrong side (if any) of the appropriate fabric, matching grain lines. Draw around it with a sharp pencil, *remembering to transfer the balance marks.* Keep your pencil sharp. Continue until all the pieces are marked, leaving at least ½ in/1.2 cm between them. Cut them out, adding approximately ¼ in/6 mm seam allowance to all edges. You should have 18 groups of pieces for the light blocks and 18 for the dark ones. (Working on a fine sandpaper board keeps small pieces of fabric still and will help you to be more accurate as you draw around templates.)

6 Keeping the small diagram in front of you, as a guide to positioning, lay out the pieces of the block, wrong side up. When piecing, I prefer first to join individual pieces into pairs, completing all the work – pinning, tacking, stitching, checking and pressing – before joining the pairs into larger units.

First pin the pieces together through the pencil line at each end. (Where this is at a straight side, pin vertically and leave these pins in place while you machine stitch. This prevents the edges from going askew.) Continue pinning along the line, matching up balance marks so that the curves will fit evenly together, then tack (see diagram 2). On a tight convex curve, as in the black quarter circle, cut "V"s out of the seam allowance to reduce bulk, cutting close to the pencil line, but not through it. The matching, concave curve will need snipping to allow it to stretch (see diagram 3). It is best to machine stitch with the concave curve on top.

Tack together pieces 3 and 9, 7 and 8, 1 and 2, 4 and 5, 6 and 7. Machine stitch, using a neutral thread. Check, and if you have swerved off the line, re-stitch. Remove the tacking, and press the seams towards the curve. Next tack together pieces 2 and 3, 5 and 6, as before, finally 3 and 4.

2

3

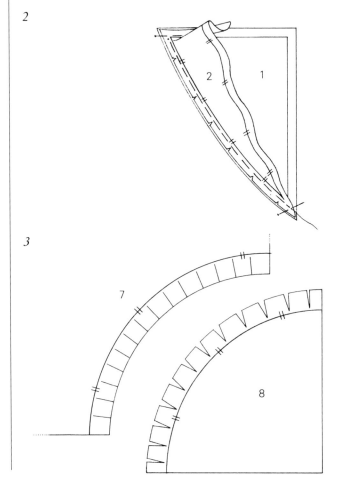

7 Press the work on the wrong side with a steam iron. Some seams will lie one way, others the opposite. They usually curve naturally the way they should be pressed, but if a dark seam allowance shows through, persuade it to lie the other way. Running the point of the iron along the stitching to make the seam allowance stand up before pressing it flat gives a crisp line. Finally, press the work on the right side.

8 Check each block as you complete it to make sure it is 12 in/30.5 cm square. If not, lay your templates over the work to see where it has gone wrong! This may seem like extra trouble, but even more trouble will result from inaccurate blocks.

9 Make up 36 blocks and join them as shown in diagram 4. Then trim the edges as shown to leave partial blocks 7 in/18 cm wide. Or, if you are using half-blocks for the edges, make up the required 26 blocks; cut 2 light and 2 dark blocks in half vertically; cut 2 light and 2 dark in half horizontally; cut 1 of each into quarters. Join these partial blocks as shown in diagram 4, taking special care to match the design as in the main section. Two each of the light and dark quarters will be left over.

Adding the borders

1 For the inner (shocking pink) border, cut strips 2½ in/6.5 cm wide, and join them to make 2 strips, each 62½ in/159 cm long, and 2 measuring 67 in/170 cm long. Take the shorter 2 of the 4 strips, and fold and crease them at the halfway point and quarter-way points. Similarly crease the edges of the quilt top on the corresponding edges. Place the border strip on the quilt, right sides facing and edges matching; match and pin the fold marks together. Work along the edge, easing the quilt into the border as you pin. The sides may have stretched a little; if necessary, put in lots of pins at right angles, so that you can machine stitch over them. Stitch with the quilt top uppermost in order to control the seam allowances. Repeat on the opposite edge of the quilt. Then join the longer borders to the remaining sides. Check the work and press the seams towards the border.

2 The grey border inset with bright pink curves demands concentration, so beginners should be aware of this before tackling it. A plain grey border can be substituted. To make the pieced border, cut the grey fabric into 8 strips, each 3¾ in/9.5 cm wide, across the width of the fabric. (This width will give you ½ in/1.2 cm seam

4

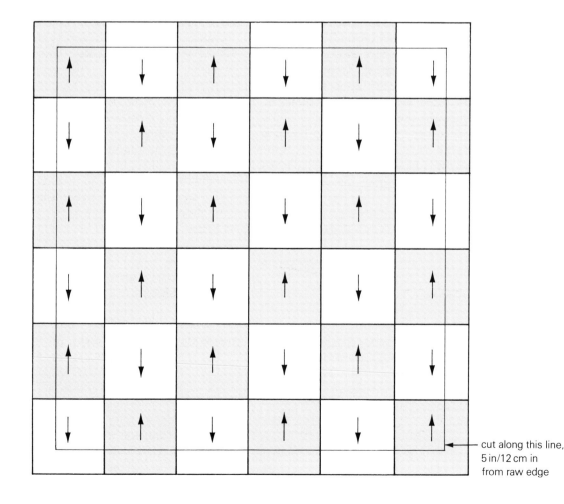

cut along this line, 5 in/12 cm in from raw edge

allowance on the outside – an extra ¼ in/6 mm in case you need to straighten the edge after quilting.) Temporarily join the strips into pairs, either tacking or machine stitching; this join will be replaced by one of the pink wavy stripes. You now have 4 grey border strips, each 90½ in/230 cm long.

3 Cut a strip of tracing paper 3 × 12 in/7.5 × 30.5 cm. Place it over the tracing of the complete block, along one of the edges including the bright pink curve, and trace this section of the curve. Write "edge" along the edge. Roughly colour the curve so that it will show up.

4 Place the patchwork wrong side up. Lay one of the grey strips next to the shocking pink border. Adjust it if necessary, so that the join is positioned where the pink curve will emerge. Pin the strip to the pink border, overlapping the edges by ¼ in/6 mm, to hold the two edges together.

Lay the 12 in/30.5 cm complete tracing over a block where the bright pink curve would logically emerge, aligning the tracing carefully with the patchwork. Slip the border tracing under the block tracing, aligning their respective pink strips; then remove the latter carefully. Slip a small piece of dressmaker's carbon under the bright pink area (see diagram 5), and use the wheel to mark the curved edges on the grey fabric. These are the *stitching lines*. For the cutting lines, mark the grey fabric again, ¼ in/6 mm inside these lines. Mark the ends of the *stitching* lines on the edge of the pink fabric, with a small snip or a pencil mark. These marks will show you where to position the grey border strips.

Repeat, marking 3 curves on the grey strip for each side. Note that the grey border should be joined in the same sequence as the pink one, so that shorter grey strips are joined to the shorter pink strips.

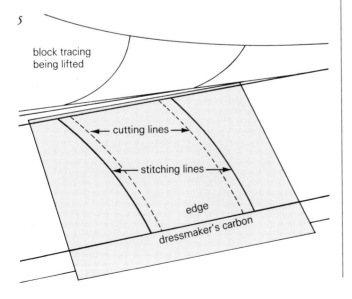

5

block tracing being lifted

← cutting lines →

← stitching lines →

edge

dressmaker's carbon

5 Cut out the pink section from the small tracing, and use this to make a cardboard template for the pink shape; add seam allowances. Write "edge" on the edge corresponding to the same one on the tracing. Cut out 12 bright pink curves, placing "edge" on the straight grain. Sew the bright pink curves into the grey border, first cutting the grey strip along the marked cutting lines.

6 Pin the shorter grey borders onto the corresponding sides of the pink border, matching the pink curves to the marks on the pink border (made in step 4). Machine stitch, with the grey border uppermost. Trim off the excess at the corners. Repeat on the longer sides. Press the work very well.

Quilting and Finishing

1 You can quilt only "in-the-ditch", if you like, or also through the various pieces, as we did. In any case, none of the lines should be more than 4 in/10 cm apart.

Plan your quilting design on the full-size tracing of the block (unless you are simply quilting along the seams); then place the tracing over the work and transfer the lines using a wheel and dressmaker's carbon.

2 Cut and join the wadding, if necessary, to make a piece approximately 73 in/185 cm square. Cut and join the backing fabric to make a piece approximately 74 in/188 cm square; this includes a margin for binding the edges.

3 Lay the backing, wrong side up, on a large table or on the floor, and smooth it out. Without stretching, hold the sides in position with pieces of masking tape. Lay the wadding over the backing, centring it. Put the top, right side up, on top, again checking that it is centred. Pin a line through the centre, top to bottom and side to side. Tack, fairly densely (preferably using diagonal tacking) from the centre outwards, covering a quarter of the area at a time.

4 You can work the quilting on a frame, as we did, or over your hand. Start in the middle and work out towards the edges.

5 When you have finished quilting, trim the edges, if necessary, to straighten them. Bring the backing fabric to the front – first on two opposite sides, then on the others – turn under the raw edges, and slipstitch the edges to the grey border. We cut a bright pink strip 1¼ in/3.2 cm wide on the straight grain, machine stitched it in place, folded and slipstitched it to the back. For this binding you will need extra fabric.

Don't forget to put a label with your name and the date on the back of the quilt.

Christmas Decorations

Hilkka Dorey

Hilkka Dorey has had a love of needlework since childhood. A Finn married to an Englishman, she has lived in Buckinghamshire for over thirty years. She has been teaching various aspects of needlework, particularly patchwork and quilting, at local adult education centres for over twelve years, and is also a regular tutor at the Missenden Abbey summer schools. Her workshops on Christmas fabric decorations are very popular.

As a child, living on a remote farm in Finland, Hilkka made Christmas decorations using paper, straw, wood shavings, fir cones and other locally available materials. Today she applies modern needlecraft techniques to some of the basic methods she used then.

Sources and Approaches

I am always looking for designs and ideas in non-needlework media that can be adapted for needlework techniques. Christmas decorations of the type I made in Finland as a child were usually made of paper and wood shavings, but now that fabric can be stiffened with Bondaweb (transfer fusing web) it is possible to reproduce these decorations in fabric. I also incorporate traditional patchwork patterns in some of my designs. The wide range of American Christmas print fabrics is a rich source of ideas; I have acquired many of these prints and have experimented extensively with them.

Every year I make new decorations in preparation for my Christmas workshops, and I now have a very large collection of them. I am often asked where I hang all the decorations. In fact, it is impossible to hang them all up, so only a selection is used. I am always sorry when Christmas is over and the decorations and fabrics are put away for another year.

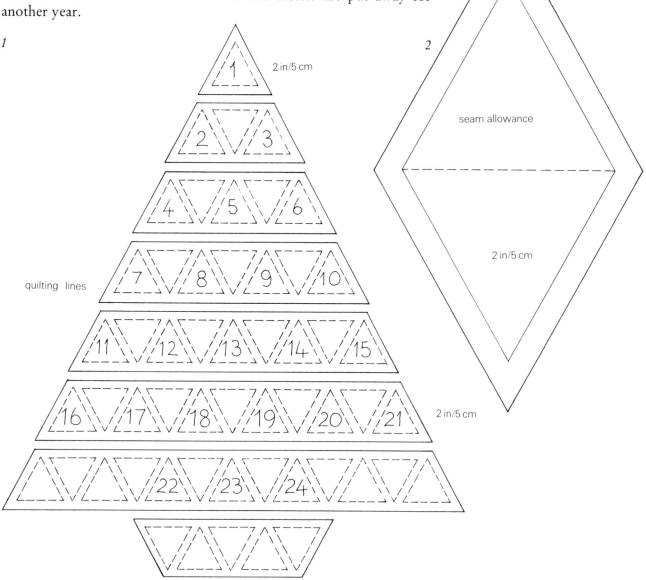

I have chosen seven items for this workshop: a small plaited wreath for hanging on the tree, a quilted Advent calendar tree, a door decoration woven in a heart shape, a scented hanging composed of three padded hearts, a snowflake tree decoration, a folded-star patchwork hanging and a hanging made in "stained glass" appliqué.

Advent Tree

This quilted Advent calendar tree (shown in the photograph on page 136) is based on an equilateral triangle. The tree is quilted with triangular padded shapes which serve as the windows. It makes an attractive hanging during the Advent period, when a triangular window is opened each day.

The tree is about 16 in/40 cm high; each window measures 2¼ in/5.7 cm on a side.

Materials

For main tree and backing, green cotton fabric, any width: ⅝ yard/50 cm
For padded flaps, red cotton fabric, 36 in/90 cm wide: ⅜ yard/30 cm
Lightweight (2-ounce) wadding: piece 22 in/50 cm square: ⅝ yard/50 cm
Calico (prewashed): ⅝ yard/50 cm
Sew-Away waste canvas, or ordinary single mesh needlepoint canvas with 12 threads to 1 in/2.5 cm
Red stranded embroidery floss
White lace or broderie anglaise, 1 in/2.5 cm wide: 1⅞ yards/1.6 metres
Small piece of narrow green ribbon
Red beads, ⅛ in/4 mm in diameter
Drawing and sewing materials (see page 10)
Dressmaker's carbon

To Make the Tree

1 Enlarge the pattern (diagram 1) to the required size (see page 42). Cut out the individual strips and use them to cut strips of the green fabric and the calico, adding ¼ in/6 mm seam allowance.

2 Transfer the quilting lines onto each strip of fabric.

3 Place a small piece of the canvas over each space for a date (see diagram 1), and embroider the appropriate number in cross stitch, using the canvas threads as a grid. Use 1 strand of the embroidery floss. Damp the canvas and carefully pull out the canvas threads.

4 Make up a "sandwich" of each strip, wadding and calico, and quilt along the marked lines, using a single strand of floss.

5 Trace the diamond (diagram 2), and use this template to cut 24 red diamonds. Cut the template in half, and use it to cut 24 half triangles from wadding.

6 Fold each diamond in half into a triangle (see diagram 3a) and place a wadding triangle on top. Stitch along one raw edge of the triangle through all thicknesses (see diagram 3b). Trim the seam allowances close to the stitching, and turn the triangles right side out.

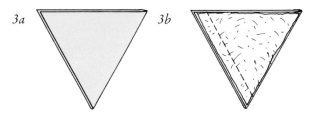

3a   *3b*

7 Work a small thread loop on the point of each triangle opposite the raw edges.

8 When all the triangles have been made up, tack them to the green strips in the spaces between the dates (see diagram 4).

4

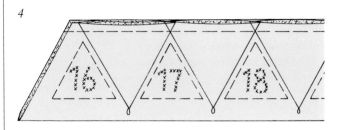

9 Tack and machine stitch all the green strips together to form the tree.

10 Using the completed tree as a pattern, trace around it onto the other piece of green fabric. Cut this out, adding seam allowances to all edges.

11 Gather the lace to fit the edges of the tree (see photograph). Machine stitch it to the right side of the padded tree, with the decorative edge inwards, and raw edges matching.

12 Fold under the edge (thus turning the lace outwards), and tack it in place. Also turn under and tack the seam allowance of the backing. Tack the two pieces together, and slipstitch around all edges.

13 Sew a bead "button" to each intersection of the triangles. Sew a ribbon loop to the top of the tree. Fasten all the red padded triangles over the numbers. Turn them down during Advent, to reveal the dates.

Woven Heart Door Decoration

As a child I used to make woven heart baskets in wood shavings to be filled with greenery and hung on the door. My fabric version is easier to construct, as the fabric strips are more pliable than the wood shavings. They are fused with Bondaweb zigzag-stitched around the edges, then woven.

The heart measures approximately 6 in/15 cm high and 8 in/20 cm wide.

Materials

2 contrasting Christmas prints, or other suitable fabric, 36 in/90 cm wide: ⅜ yard/30 cm
Red or green bias binding, ½ in/1.2 cm wide: ¾ yard/ 60 cm
Red and green ribbon, ⅛ in/3 mm wide: ½ yard/40 cm
Bondaweb (transfer fusing web): piece approximately 12 in/30 cm square
Drawing and sewing materials (see page 10)

To Make the Basket

1 Cut each of the two fabrics in half crosswise (parallel to selvedges). Fuse the matching halves with the Bondaweb. The two fabrics will be called "A" and "B".

2 From each fabric cut 8 strips, each ¾ in/2 cm wide and 11 in/28 cm long, and 3 strips the same width but 7 in/18 cm long. Zigzag stitch or blanket stitch along all edges to prevent fraying.

3 Fold each strip in half and press the fold. Take one long strip of fabric A and fabric B and loop them together at the folds (see diagram 5a). Take another long strip of fabric A, and loop it over strip B, this time over

the farther side of the strip (diagram 5b). Take a long strip of B and loop it over both fabric A strips (see diagram 5c). Continue in this way until you have woven all the longer strips together.

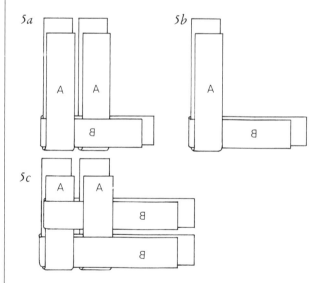

4 Complete the heart shape by weaving in the shorter strips, 3 on a side.

5 Trim the ends of the strips to make a smooth shape, and tack them together to hold them in place. Stitch bias binding over them.

6 Tie the two lengths of narrow ribbon together to form a bow (first cutting off a little for a hanging loop), and sew it in place at the centre of one side of the heart. Sew the loop to the same point on the other side. Fill the heart with sprigs of greenery.

Folded Patchwork Hanging

This hanging uses the familiar patchwork technique known as Folded Star, or Somerset patchwork. This technique produces a kaleidoscopic effect, creating a number of star shapes. Hardly any sewing is needed; the shapes are folded and glued in place, then machine stitched down the centre. The following instructions are for a basic star shape.

Each star measures approximately 4 in/10 cm in diameter (see photograph on page 137).

Materials

Small quantities of 3 Christmas prints (light background, red print, green print) or other suitable fabrics
A square of calico or old sheet for foundation fabric
Glue stick
Transparent nylon thread
Red or green bias binding, ½ in/1.2 cm wide: 1⅛ yards/ 1 metre, or 1¾ yards/1.5 metres narrow lace
Red or green ribbon, ¾ in/2 cm wide: ⅞ yard/80 cm
Narrow ribbon, ⅛ in/3 mm wide: 1¾ yards/1.5 metres
3 brass bells
Brass ring
Squares of red or green felt for backing
Drawing and sewing materials (see page 10) including a protractor

To Make the Hanging

1 For each star shape, cut 3 strips in the chosen fabric, one 1¼ × 8 in/3.2 × 20 cm for the centre patches and the others 1¼ × 16 in/3.2 × 40 cm. Press under ¼ in/6 mm on one long edge of each strip, then cut it into 2 in/5 cm-long rectangles.

2 From the calico, cut a circle 4 in/10 cm in diameter. With a pencil, ruler and protractor, divide it into eighths. Make sure that all angles are 45°.

3 Fold the rectangles into triangles as shown (see diagram 6), using a little adhesive on the fold to hold the

6

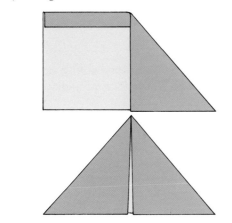

corners in place. Press the triangles (it is quite safe to iron them); this will improve their appearance.

4 *Round One* Place the inner 4 triangles on the marked lines at the centre of the circle, folded side up and with their points touching (see diagram 7). Apply a little adhesive to the back of each to hold it in place.

7

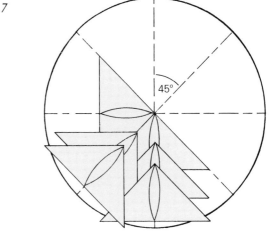

5 *Round Two* Take 8 folded triangles and place them ½ in/1.2 cm from the centre, on top of the triangles in Round One and on the lines between (see diagram 7).

6 *Round Three* Take the remaining 8 folded triangles and place them on top of the Round Two triangles and a good ⅜ in/9 mm away from the points. N.B. The folded triangles will not cover the entire outside edge of the foundation material – this will be done by the bias binding or lace.

7 Trim the edges of the outer triangles along the edge of the foundation circle. Cut a circle of felt the same size, and place the patchwork circle on top. Machine stitch, using invisible sewing thread, down the centre channels of the patches.

8 Stitch bias binding over the edges, or cut a length of lace one and a half times the circumference of the circle, gather it up to fit the edge, and sew it in place.

9 Make 2 more stars in the same way.

10 Attach the stars, evenly spaced, on the ¾ in/2 cm ribbon. Cut the narrow ribbon into 3 equal lengths; thread on the bells, and tie them around the hanging ribbon in bows as shown. Loop the main ribbon over the brass ring and sew it in place.

Snowflake Tree Decoration

Most of us as children have made snowflakes by folding and cutting paper. I have tried to recapture the beauty of the snowflakes I remember from the hard, crisp winters of my childhood in Finland. These delicate cutwork snowflakes are made of two layers of fabric bonded together and zigzagged around the edges.

The snowflake measures approximately 5 in/12.5 cm in diameter (see photograph on page 136).

Materials

White machine embroidery thread or fine sewing thread
Sheer white fabric (preferably with a sparkle in it), any width: ⅜ yard/30 cm
Fine crochet thread and hook
Bondaweb (transfer fusing web)
Drawing and sewing equipment (see page 10), including very sharp embroidery scissors

To Make the Snowflake

1 Take a piece of paper a little over 5 in/13 cm square, and fold it in half, then into quarters and then into eighths (see diagram 8).

8

2 Using paper scissors, cut a lacy design in the folded paper (you may wish to draw this first). Open out the snowflake pattern.

3 Cut 2 × 10 in/25 cm squares of the fabric. Fuse them together, using Bondaweb and a cool iron. Iron carefully to get rid of all the ripples.

4 Trace the design from the paper pattern onto the sheer fabric using a marking pencil.

5 Slightly loosen the upper thread tension on your machine, and set the machine to a narrow satin stitch. Stitch along all drawn lines. With the embroidery scissors trim away the surplus fabric and holes in the design, taking care not to cut the stitching.

6 Crochet a hanging loop, and tie or sew it to the top of the decoration.

Small Plaited Wreath

These small plaited wreaths make attractive tree ornaments. They are made out of three stuffed tubes plaited together and formed into a ring.

The completed ring measures approximately 3¼ in/8 cm in diameter (see photograph on page 137).

Materials

3 contrasting fabrics, preferably Christmas prints: a piece at least 9 in/23 cm long of each
Small amount of knitting yarn, rug yarn or cord
Red and green ribbon, ⅛ in/3 mm wide, for bow: approximately ½ yard/50 cm of each
Small brass bell
Drawing and sewing materials (see page 10)

To Make the Wreath

1 Cut three strips, each 1 × 9 in/2.5 × 23 cm, from each fabric.

2 Fold each strip in half lengthwise, right side inside, and machine stitch the long edges together, taking about ⅛ in/3 mm seam allowance, to form a long tube. Leave long threads from the stitching.

3 Thread a large darning needle with the thread ends, and take it through the tube, turning it right side out. Stuff the tubes with yarn, using the darning needle.

4 Place the three tubes side by side, and join them by oversewing them at one end. Plait the tubes and sew the ends together to form into a ring.

5 Make a bow from red and green ribbon, and attach with bell to the join.

Three-Heart Hanging

Hearts are a symbol of good will. This three-heart hanging, stuffed with Christmas potpourri will add a lovely fragrance to the home.

The larger hearts measure approximately 3½ in/9 cm in height; the smaller ones, 2 in/5 cm.

Materials

Small pieces of 3 different red prints, preferable with heart designs
Red and green ribbon, ⅛ in/3 mm wide: approximately 1½ yards/1.3 metres
Red or green ribbon, ⅝ in/1.5 cm wide, with picot edging: ⅝ yard/50 cm

Narrow lace: 1½ yards/1.4 metres
Christmas potpourri
3 small jingle bells
Brass ring for hanging
Drawing and sewing materials (see page 10)

To Make the Hanging

1 Fold a sheet of paper in half, and draw 2 half heart shapes on the fold: one 3½ in/9 cm tall and the other 2 in/5 cm tall. Cut around both shapes and open out the heart patterns.

2 Cut 2 large hearts and 2 small hearts from each of the chosen fabrics.

3 Cut the lace into 3 equal lengths. Gather each length to fit the edges of the large heart. Tack it to the right side of one heart with raw edges matching (see diagram 9).

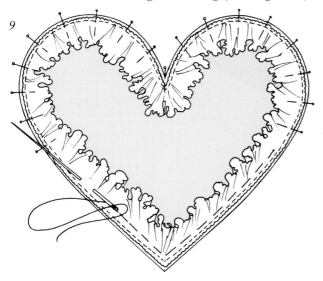

4 Place the matching heart shape, right side down, on top, and tack around the edges through all three layers. Stitch around the edge, taking ¼ in/6 mm seam allowance and leaving a gap of about 1 in/3 cm on one side.

5 Turn the heart right side out, carefully pushing out the point and smoothing the edges. Stuff the shape with potpourri, then slipstitch the opening edges together.

6 Make the small hearts following steps 4 and 5. Make 3 double bows in the narrow ribbon, threading a bell onto the centre of each. Sew a small heart and bow to the top of each larger heart.

7 Sew each double heart to the wide ribbon, spacing them evenly and leaving a few inches/centimetres at top and bottom. Attach the brass ring for hanging, and trim the end of the ribbon neatly as shown in the photograph.

Stained Glass Appliqué Hanging

This hanging uses the popular technique of "stained glass" appliqué to create an attractive Christmas hanging. The black bias strips applied over the raw edges of the different fabrics suggest the leading on a stained glass window.

The hanging measures approximately 13 in/33 cm in diameter.

Materials

For the foundation and backing, calico (prewashed): ½ yard/40 cm

Scraps of Christmas prints for border and candle

Scraps of yellow and gold material for the flame and its glow

Scraps of red and green material for berries and holly leaves

Lightweight (2-ounce) polyester wadding: 16 in/40 cm square

Black ½ in/1.2mm bias binding for "lead": approximately 5½ yards/5 metres

Scraps of black fabric for the berries

Glue stick

Drawing and sewing materials (see page 10)

To Make the Hanging

1 Enlarge the design (see diagram 10) on paper to the required size – 13 in/33 cm diameter in this case. (Adjust the fabric quantities to suit if another size is required.) Go over the lines with a dark felt-tip pen.

2 Place the foundation fabric on top of the design, and trace the design onto the foundation fabric with a pencil or marking pen. Make another tracing for templates.

3 Use the templates to cut out the shapes in the selected fabrics. Add seam allowances ¼ in/6 mm only to those edges on the circumference of the hanging.

4 Position all the cut-out pieces on the foundation fabric, and pin them in place. Tack as close as possible along the edges with black sewing thread.

5 Prepare the bias binding. Wash it to remove starch, in warm water and dishwashing liquid. Rinse and allow the binding to dry. Iron it flat to remove the folds. Fold the binding in half lengthwise and machine stitch along the raw edges, close to the edge (see diagram 11a). Turn under the raw edges and tack through all thicknesses (see diagram 11b), using white threads (easily seen and removed). The "lead" is now narrow and flexible enough to be applied.

10

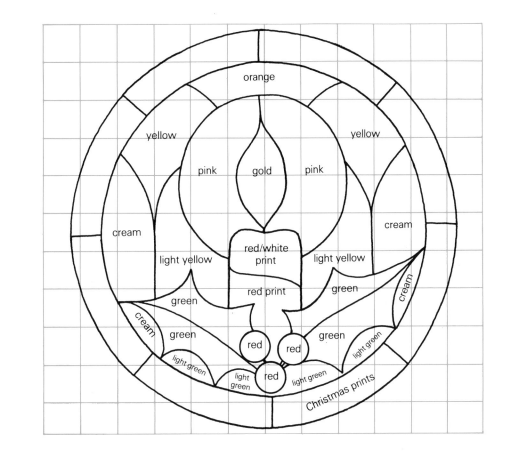

11a

11b

12

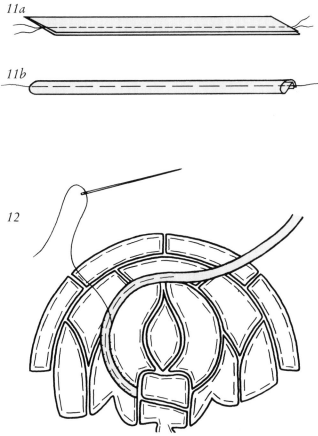

6 Before applying the binding, study the design and determine the positioning of the lead – which lines go over, which under. Tack the prepared binding into position with white thread. Slipstitch along both sides of the binding with invisible stitches (see diagram 12). Continue in this way until all the binding has been applied. Remove all tacking threads.

A slightly different technique is required for the berries, because of their small size. Trace the "red" circles onto paper and cut them out. Apply a dab of glue stick to one side of the circles and stick them onto the wrong side of the red material; cut out the berries leaving ¼ in/ 6 mm turning allowance. Tack the edges under. Trace the larger surrounding circles, and use these tracings to cut circles of black fabric, again adding ¼ in/6 mm. Centre the berries on the black circles, and slipstitch them in place. Remove tacking; cut a small slit in the black fabric and pull out the paper circle. Turn under and tack the edges of the black circle. Slipstitch the berries to the hanging. Place the work on the wadding and backing and tack across it in several places.

7 Using thread to match the fabrics, quilt around the shapes.

8 Trim the edge of the circle, and bind with a strip of bias binding, making a loop at the top for hanging.

Colourwash

Deirdre Amsden

After studying at the Cambridge School of Art, Deirdre Amsden pursued a career as a freelance illustrator for fifteen years. A short embroidery course at the Victoria and Albert Museum, London, in 1974 awakened her interest in quilting and patchwork. Thereafter her transition from illustration to quiltmaking was self-taught. Deirdre Amsden's work has appeared regularly in exhibitions and books. Since the mid-1980s she has specialized in designing her "Colourwash" quilts, in which she explores value contrasts, illusions of transparency and three-dimensional effects.

Sources and Approaches

While visiting my mother in the early 1970s, I became interested in a patchwork competition she had entered. She suggested I enter the competition too and shared her pieces of printed fabric with me. I disliked the patterns, so I cut the material into 1½ in/4 cm squares, sorted them into light, medium and dark values and sewed them into what I now realize was a "Sunshine and Shadow" arrangement, with the lightest square in the centre, shading to dark and back to light, and so on. Once I left my mother's encouraging guidance the patchwork lay unfinished, and the idea of shading patches of fabric into one another lay dormant until I took up quiltmaking full-time.

I taught myself quiltmaking from books, avidly consuming one after another and learning a little more from each. I began to question the conventional wisdom that fabrics must contrast and that quilting should be used to outline the patchwork design. Harking back to my piece of unfinished patchwork, I thought about blending patterned fabrics together and grading the patches from one value, or colour, to another. Quilting across the patchwork seams, I surmised, would further blur the patchwork shapes.

Colourwash Stripes I, II and III

Before embarking on these three quilts I had made several smaller striped pieces. All three designs contain strong vertical stripes, and all include both squares and right-angled triangles. In the first (see previous page), the stripes are intersected at regular intervals to create a symmetrical design of elongated hexagons with a zigzag strip at top and bottom. The stripes of the second (left) are cross-cut at random, forming an asymmetrical variation of the first. The tension of the quilting stitches, snaking diagonally across this quilt in one direction only, distorts the way it hangs. I have partly remedied the problem by washing the quilt and pinning it out to shape while it dried, but designing some lines of quilting to run in the opposite direction would have balanced the tension more effectively.

The third design is more complex (see detail, right). I introduced a second, less acute, angle and progressed from lightest on the left side to darkest on the right. The stripes now appear as bars, through which rhomboid shapes are visible. The hand quilting runs diagonally from top right to bottom left, following one angle, and crosses the machine quilting (following the direction of the second angle) in the central rhomboids.

Colourwash Stripes I, 57½ × 87 in/146 × 221 cm; II, 53 × 74 in/135 × 188 cm; III, 48 × 80½ in/122 × 204 cm

◀ Colourwash Cubes II and III ▶

These two quilts were made as a pair for two American colleagues and their wives, who wanted similar-but-different hangings. The commission came about after a visit to an exhibition of my quilts in St. Ives, Cornwall. They liked a large, regular cube design but wanted something smaller in scale. The idea for the cubes of varying sizes was inspired by a quilting design I had used on a previous quilt. To achieve the similar-but-different aspect I changed the direction of the cubes. Also, I shaded "Cubes II" (right) from dark to light diagonally across the quilt (as a result some fabrics acted as light in one corner, moved through medium in the central area, to emerge as dark in the opposite corner), but I kept a strong contrast between the three values in "Cubes III" (see detail, left). The brief also stipulated that the quilts should have no "top" and "bottom"; hanging sleeves on all four sides enable them to be hung any way up.

Colourwash Cubes II, 64 × 53 in/ 163 × 132 cm; III, 60 × 50 in/152 × 127 cm

These ideas took shape one day when I was offered a large box of scraps from a friend's dress design business. I was excitedly rummaging through an array of Liberty prints when I noticed how well they blended together. I cut a square from each pattern and colourway, which I then graded from the darkest values at the top down to the palest at the bottom. This arrangement reminded me of an art school exercise in which one attempts to lay a smooth wash of watercolour paint across the paper without a blotch or tidemark spoiling the surface. Hence the name "Colourwash". I quilted this first piece (a crib quilt) in a simple diamond pattern. My first series of "Colourwash" pieces were all variations on this theme.

In the second series, a few years later, I reintroduced contrast, which resulted in striped, framed and quartered designs. Both series were small-scale pieces made from patterned Liberty lawn.

Later still I began using a wider range of fabrics and mixing dress-weight fabrics and lightweight furnishing fabrics, pure cottons and polyester-cottons, and a greater variety of prints, adding stripes, checks, spots and so on to the ubiquitous floral patterns. These more robust fabrics increased my palette and enlarged the scale of my work. I have learned to appreciate unusual and even hideous fabrics, as they often provide a colour transition or "splat" in an otherwise smooth wash of colour and contribute to a richer surface effect. Scattering the

Colourwash Framed X
(overleaf)

Only small-scale prints are used in this miniature hanging, which suggests a garden seen through a window. The patches measure ³/₄ in/2 cm square. The diagonal quilting across the "window panes" changes to a diamond pattern in the "frame" areas.

11 × 14 in/28 × 35 cm

ugly among the beautiful – so that only close inspection will reveal, for example, a common gingham snuggling up to an elegant fashion fabric, or Popeye sandwiched between a sizzling African print and a Javanese batik – amuses me and feels liberating.

When designing I am aware of the minute and busy detail produced by the myriad patterned fabrics, so I strive to simplify the overall design. I aim to create a strong image which gradually dissolves and disappears into a splatter of pattern as the viewer approaches for a closer look and which re-emerges only when he or she stands back. The photographs on these pages demonstrate this effect by showing a close-up detail of one of the quilts and a complete view of another in the same series.

It continues to surprise me how a simple idea, employing simple construction techniques, has gradually developed over the years until it now demands my full attention and will probably continue to do so for the foreseeable future.

A Colourwash Wallhanging

This workshop explains and illustrates the process of designing and making a colourwash quilt. You can use the instructions either to make a wallhanging similar to the one shown or to design an original hanging of your own.

The wallhanging shown above is entitled "Colourwash Framed IX". Here, the patches have been arranged to create an optical illusion: all of the values, from light to dark, appear to recede in the area around the frame, but to advance within it, so that it seems to float in space. The hand quilting in the centre section and the machine quilting in the outer section cross each other in the "floating" frame.

The hanging measures 23 in/58 cm square.

Materials

For the patchwork, a minimum of 30 different fabrics, more if possible, in each of 4 value ranges (dark, medium-dark, medium-light and light), making a total of at least 120 different fabrics – only small amounts are needed

For backing fabric of any width: ¾ yard/70 cm

For binding, a fabric of any width (can be the same as backing): ¼ yard/30 cm (for a double binding)

Lightweight (2-ounce) wadding: ¾ yard/70 cm

Lace pins

2 wooden battens, approximately ¾ in/2 cm wide and 22 in/56 cm long

2 screw eyes

Flannel board (optional)

Drawing and sewing materials (see page 10)

Three Design Fundamentals: Value, Colour and Texture

Value is the degree of lightness or darkness that defines the design. Contrast and balance between the value placements are of primary importance when designing patchwork. Depth and spatial qualities are determined by value contrasts. In most cases, light values advance and dark ones recede. However, dark shapes silhouetted against a light background will advance. Illusions of transparency and three-dimensionality are created by value placements; the most familiar example of this is "Tumbling Blocks" patchwork (see pages 96–103). Having established the value placements, you can then translate them into colour with your choice of fabrics.

Colour evokes an emotional response in the viewer. Colours are intensely personal; they suggest mood and atmosphere and can manipulate our feelings. Colours are not static; they are influenced by light and shade and surrounding colours; they change with the time of day and under artificial light. Unlike painters, patchworkers rarely deal with pure colour. The weave, weight and composition of cloth all have a bearing on its colour, as do printed and woven patterns. Don't be intimidated by colour – have fun experimenting with colour and fabric.

Texture, both visual and tactile, is available for exploitation by the quiltmaker. Printed fabrics differ texturally; a tiny geometric print, for example, is texturally different from a voluptuous floral, even though it may not feel different. Satin and velvet both feel and look different. Additional texture is provided by the quilting. If the patchwork and quilting are designed concurrently they are more likely to complement each other than if the quilting is designed later.

Designing the Work

1 Start by making rough pencil sketches to indicate value placements, shading and overall shape of the project (see diagram 1).

1

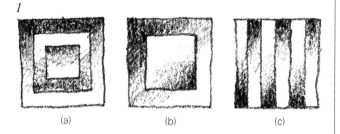

(a)   (b)   (c)

2 Select the most interesting sketch and transfer it to squared or isometric paper (according to choice of template shape). Here, I have chosen 1a, and have decided to use a square template. Diagram 2 shows the design trans-

ferred to a grid in which each square represents 1½ inches. (You could, instead, use centimetres as your unit of measurement.)

2

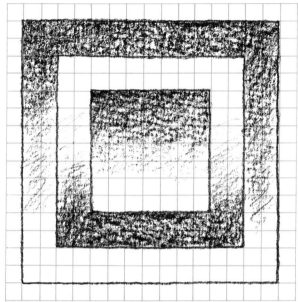

3 Lay a sheet of tracing paper over the design drawing. Draw a quilting pattern on the tracing paper and see how it relates to the patchwork design. Try several of these, if necessary, until you have one that you like. Here (see diagram 3) I have chosen a diagonal grid, which in the

3

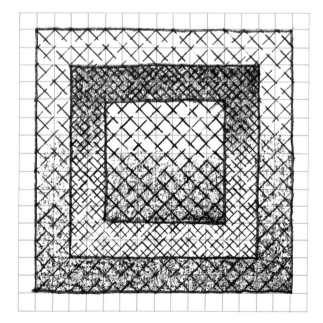

outer section crosses the patches from corner to corner but in the centre section is off-set (forming a diamond in the centre of each patch). Where the two cross, in the "floating" frame, the grid is reduced to quarter size.

The more thought you give to the design stage, the fewer the problems later. But design drawings are not etched in tablets of stone, so if a better idea occurs, while the project is underway, spend some time checking it out. Sometimes a drawing that works on paper will not translate satisfactorily into fabric without further changes – so it's back to the drawing board!

4 Decide on the size of the template(s) in relation to the overall size of the project. A square of 1½ in/3.8 cm is recommended for the illustrated project (which is 15 × 15 squares). This will produce an overall measurement of 22½ × 22½ in/57 × 57 cm. A 2 in/5 cm square would increase it to 30 × 30 in/75 × 75 cm; 1 in/2.5 cm would reduce it to 15 × 15 in/37.5 × 37.5 cm. The total number of squares required is 225 (15 × 15).

Choose a scale that is comfortable for you – some people are natural miniaturists; others prefer boldness. Bear in mind, however, that if the patch is big, blending will be more difficult to achieve with small-scale prints; conversely, large-scale prints may be impractical for small patches.

5 Cut an accurate, sturdy template for each shape in the design, to include seam allowances. For the project illustrated, cut a 2 in/5 cm square. This includes ¼ in/6 mm seam allowances and gives a finished size of 1½ in/3.8 cm.

6 Refer to your drawing (diagram 2), and count or estimate the number of patches needed for each value in the design. This design can be divided into 4 values – dark, medium-dark, medium-light and light – more or less evenly represented. Therefore 56 or 57 patches of each value (225 divided by 4) will be required. Another design might need only 3 values, as in the Colourwash Cubes quilts on pages 150 and 151.

Choosing the Fabrics

1 Gather and sort all the fabrics into value piles. For this project about 30 different fabrics will be required in each value range (more if possible). Only a small amount of each will be needed (enough to cut 2 or 3 patches). If you cut more than one patch from each fabric, make sure they are kept apart in the final arrangement. To allow for choice when arranging the patches it is necessary to cut more than will be used.

Some designs may lend themselves to a more limited range of fabrics, or to a monochromatic range (values of one colour). To extend the choice of fabrics, without

having to purchase more, consider using the reverse side where this is different. Another possibility is to let some fabrics play a dual role (for example, as a dark and a medium-dark). Also large-scale prints may contain several quite different tonal values and thus yield patches for more than one value range.

Over-dyeing and tea-dyeing commercially printed fabrics is another option. Experiment with surplus or garish prints that might benefit from being toned down, so that not too much has been sacrificed if the results are disappointing.

2 Prepare the fabrics as described on page 11 (unless the work will be dry-cleaned) to shrink them and re-move surplus dyestuffs. Discard any fabric that violently discolours the water.

3 Press the fabrics while still damp, and stack them in neat piles ready for marking and cutting out.

Cutting and Joining the Patches

1 Cut out the required number of patches from each fabric (plus extras), either using a rotary cutter and ruler or by marking around the template and cutting each one out individually. When cutting a few patches at a time from scraps of fabric the latter method tends to waste less fabric. Place templates so that pattern motifs are off centre or bleed out of the patch.

2 Lay the patches out in four rows, according to their value (see diagram 4), so that a portion of each one is visible.

4

3 Referring to the working drawing (diagram 2), start arranging the patches in the design. Begin either in the centre or at the top or bottom, or at some other point that seems logical. Either work flat on a table or vertically on a flannel board (see page 10). This stage is like doing a jigsaw puzzle. It may take several attempts to find the right patch to fit a given space. Conversely, some patches will fit into many places. Try not to be too indecisive, or the process could go on ad infinitum.

Relate patches by similarity of pattern (for example, two paisley prints) or by scale (for example, a small geometric and a small floral), or, most importantly, by colour. Try to pick up a colour in one patch and link it with a similar one in the next; for example, a yellow and green print might repeat the yellow of one neighbour and the green of another. Also take account of the colours in patches once or twice removed. Aim to balance or distribute the colours fairly evenly, unless, of course, the design dictates otherwise.

To judge if the placement of patches is satisfactory, stand well back from the work, or look down on it from a chair, and squint. Or look through the wrong end of binoculars or the viewfinder of a camera, or use a reducing glass (the opposite of a magnifying glass – available at most art shops).

4 Work out a logical sewing sequence and stick to it. By sewing pairs together first, then pairs into fours, fours into eights and so on, you will have fewer seams to

match than if the squares are sewn first into rows and the rows then sewn together. However, the former may result in a more complicated sequence than the latter.

When constructing a whole piece of patchwork from small units, without the interim stage of blocks, accuracy is essential. It may help to mark a stitching line on the wrong side, with the aid of a grid ruler (see diagram 5); this is useful whether you are sewing by hand or machine. Align the correct mark on your ruler with the lower cut edge of the patches or the seam to give a ¼ in/ 6 mm seam allowance (see diagram 5).

5 Use neutral-coloured threads to match the lightness or darkness of the fabrics – cream, ecru, dark beige, grey, brown, navy, and black. Red, maroon, mid and dark green and light blue may also be useful in some cases. To avoid re-threading the machine constantly, you can plan to sew all the pale patches at once, then all the mediums, and so on.

Press seams open to give the patchwork a flat appearance. If you wish to emphasize some areas of the design with outline quilting, then press the appropriate seams to one side. Occasionally a design may demand a seam to be pressed in two different directions (see diagram 6) or pressed towards the light value. In this case trim the seam allowance of the darker patch(es) if it shows through to the front of the work.

6

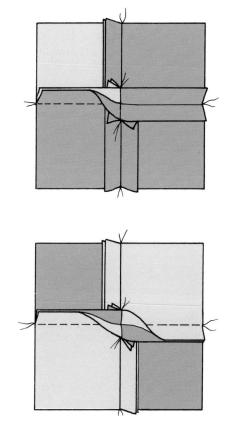

5

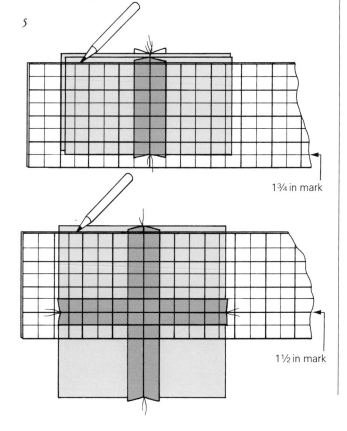

1¾ in mark

1½ in mark

To match the seams accurately, pin them together (see diagram 7). Sew right up to the pin before removing it. Lace pins, being finer than dressmakers' pins, are better for this job.

7

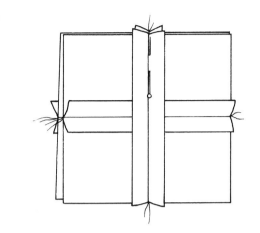

6 When the patchwork is complete, give it a final press on the wrong side, with a damp cloth, just before marking the quilting pattern.

Quilting
1 With the aid of templates or a ruler, mark out the quilting lines on the patchwork. Use sharp coloured pencils (a light and a dark) to match the colour of the quilting thread.

2 Cut the backing and wadding at least 1 in/2.5 cm larger all around than the patchwork. Pin and tack the layers together (as described on page 16) to prepare them for quilting.

3 Quilt either by hand or by machine. In some cases you may wish to combine the two, according to your own preference.

For machine quilting, slacken the pressure of the foot, enlarge the stitch size a little and check that the tension is even. The marked lines are easier to see if you use a zipper foot. Sew slowly and steadily, and to avoid puckering, always sew in the same direction as the previous lines. Quilting along the bias of the fabric layers is easier than with the straight grain.

Finishing
1 Bind the edges using a straight binding cut on the crosswise grain of the fabric. Use a double binding as described on page 17.

2 From the remaining backing fabric cut 2 strips, each 3½ in/9 cm wide and about ½ in/12 mm shorter than the width of the quilt.

Turn under the raw edges at both ends. If these hems are turned to the right side the battens can be slipped through the sleeves more easily.

3 Fold the sleeve in half lengthwise and seam (see diagram 8). Press the seam open, so that it lies along the centre of one side (see diagram 9).

8   *9*

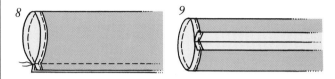

4 Centre the sleeve along the top edge of the quilt (with the raw seam edges against the quilt back), so that the top edge of the sleeve is positioned just below the binding. Pin, tack and hem the top edge of the sleeve in place, taking care not to stitch through to the front of the work.

5 Fold the sleeve up slightly so that it is now aligned with the top edge of the binding. Pin, tack and hem along the lower edge of the sleeve (see diagram 10). The sleeve will accommodate the batten without causing a bulge on the front of the hanging, also a full sleeve protects the work from the batten.

10

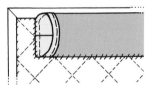

6 Make up the second sleeve in the same manner and sew to the bottom edge. This is optional but the work will hang better with a batten slipped through the lower sleeve.

7 Insert screw eyes into the top batten for hanging (see diagram 11).

11

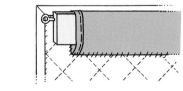

8 Sew a label, giving your name, the date and any other relevant information, to the back of the quilt, or embroider them on the front. Please remember, if adapting someone else's design or style, to give credit to the designer.

GLOSSARY

Note: Some of the terms used in this book are specific to Great Britain – equivalent descriptions are given in the definitions.

balance marks Also called "notches"; points marked on adjacent pieces of fabric to be matched when seaming in order to ensure a correct fit.

block A unit of a quilt which is made up of patched or appliquéd pieces. The blocks are repeated joined edge to edge or with alternate unpieced blocks or with sashing (see right) or on point (see below) to make up a quilt.

Bondaweb British trade name for transfer fusing web; the American trade name is Wonder-Under.

calico British name for unbleached muslin; a natural-coloured, plain-woven, medium to heavyweight cotton.

cartridge paper British term for good-quality drawing paper; may also refer to coloured paper of similar weight.

domette British name for a soft, loosely woven fabric of wool or wool and cotton, used for interlining garments or padding quilts.

Double bar stitch Two small stitches worked side by side to hold two edges or layers of fabric together.

ease To fit a longer edge of fabric to a shorter one by distributing the fullness evenly, without the use of a gathering thread.

finger-press To crease fabric between the fingers.

flat quilting To work quilting on two layers of fabric only, without a layer of padding.

free machine embroidery Embroidery worked on the machine with the presser foot removed and the feed dog lowered or covered to permit stitching in any direction.

in-the-ditch Also called "sink stitching"; quilting that is worked directly over or very close to an existing seam line.

lap quilting A method of constructing a quilt in which individual blocks are quilted, then joined.

lattice strips see under "sashing".

ombré French word meaning "shaded".

on point Describes the position of a block (see above) when it is turned so that it rests on one of the corners.

oversew British term for "overcast"; to work stitches over one or more fabric edges to join them or prevent them from fraying.

plain weave The simplest kind of weave, in which each weft thread goes alternately under and over each warp thread.

Rotary Mate Trade name for a ruler designed for use with a rotary cutter and with special markings to enable quick measuring of triangles.

sashing A pattern of plain-coloured fabric strips used between pieced blocks to join them into a quilt. Also sometimes referred to as "lattice strips".

scrap quilt A quilt made of miscellaneous fabrics, used in a random fashion throughout the design.

set The pattern in which patchwork blocks are joined.

set square British term for a right-angled triangle.

shot Term applied to fabric in which the warp and weft are of different colours, producing an iridescent effect.

sink-stitching see under "in-the-ditch".

stay-stitch To work a line of stitching along the seamline of a fabric section in order to prevent it from stretching before it is seamed.

Stitch 'n' Tear Trade name for a fabric used as a foundation, in machine embroidery and other machine techniques, which can later be torn away.

tack British term for "baste"; to work large running stitches to mark lines on a piece of fabric or hold layers together.

wadding British term for batting.

walking foot A special quilting attachment for a sewing machine, which is designed to feed the top and the bottom layers of a quilt "sandwich" through the machine evenly, thus eliminating puckering.

wholecloth quilt A quilt in which the top and bottom fabrics are a single piece of fabric. The surfaces are then completely covered with elaborate quilting patterns.

ACKNOWLEDGEMENTS

We should like to thank all the contributors for loaning their work to be photographed and we are grateful to the following photographers for the pictures of the quilts:

Jeremy Roth: pages 1, 6–7, 9, 17, 18–19, 24, 25, 27, 28, 29, 31, 44–5, 47, 48–9, 50, 51, 54–5, 56, 57, 58, 60, 69, 72–3, 74, 75, 94–5, 96, 97, 98, 104–5, 106, 107, 108, 111, 112, 114–15, 116, 117, 118, 120, 121, 122, 127, 130–1, 136–7, 140, 143, 144
Pauline Burbidge: pages 37 (top), 40
Annette Claxton: 124–5, 128, 129
John Coles: pages 32–3, 36, 37 (bottom)
Richard Hookway: cover and pages 62–3, 64, 65, 66–7, 68
Jacqui Hurst: pages 83, 86, 91
Paul Seheult: pages 146–7, 148, 149, 150, 151, 152, 153
Keith Tidball: pages 2, 34, 35, 38–9

USEFUL ADDRESSES

The Quilt Room
20 West Street, Dorking, Surrey RH4 1BL, U.K.
[Shop open 9.30 a.m. to 5.00 p.m. Monday–Saturday;
mail order and workshops]

Trudie Hughes
Patched Works Inc, 13330 Watertown Plank Road, Elm
Grove, Wisconsin 53122, U.S.A.
[Supplier of "Rotary Mate" and other quilting
equipment]

QUILTING ORGANIZATIONS

Australasia

Australian Quilters' Association
P.O. Box 297, Hawthorn, Victoria 3122, Australia

New Zealand Quilting Association
P.O. Box 5664, Dunedin, Otago, New Zealand

Tasmanian Quilting Guild
11 Balmoral Street, Sandy Bay, Tasmania 7005,
Australia

The Quilters' Guild Inc. of Australia
P.O. Box 654, Neutral Bay, N.S.W. 2089, Australia

West Australian Quilters' Guild
P.O. Box 188, Subiaco, Western Australia 6008,
Australia

U.K. & Ireland

The Quilters' Guild
OP 66, Dean Clough, Halifax, West Yorkshire HX3
5AX, U.K.

National Patchwork Association
P.O. Box 300, Hethersett, Norwich, Norfolk NR9
3DB, U.K.

Irish Patchwork Society
P.O. Box 45, Blackrock, Co. Dublin, Ireland

Rest of Europe

Patchworkgruppe Wien
Grosse Mohrengasse 27/14, A-1020 Wien, Austria

Belgische Quilteers Vereniging
Dorpsstraat 43, 3078 Meerbeek, Belgium

Dansk Patchwork Forening
Peter Toftsvej 1, 6000 Kolding, Denmark

L'Association Française du Patchwork
BP 40, 75261 Paris, France

Patchwork-Gilde
Bungersweg 6a, 2000 Hamburg 52, Germany

Quiltersgilde
Stationplein 38, 3818 LE Amersfoort, The Netherlands

Norsk Quilte Forbund
Postboks 195, Ulvoya, 0139 Oslo 1, Norway

Kviltforeningen Rikstacket
Renlavsgangen 28, 135 35 Tyreso, Sweden

Patchquilt
Postfach 55, CH-8024, Zurich, Switzerland

North America

American Quilter's Society
P.O. Box 3290, Paducah, Kentucky 42002-3290, U.S.A.

American/International Quilt Association
14520 Memorial #54, Houston, Texas 77079, U.S.A.

Canadian Quilters' Association
P.O. Box 22010, Herongate Postal Outlet, Ottawa,
Ontario, KIV 0C2, Canada

National Quilting Association Inc
P.O. Box 393, Ellicott City, Maryland 21043-0393,
U.S.A.

INDEX